# ZEN AND THE BIRDS OF APPETITE

*With no bird singing*
*The mountain is yet more still.*

ZEN SAYING

*Ride your horse along the edge of the sword*
*Hide yourself in the middle of the flames*
*Blossoms of the fruit tree will bloom in the fire*
*The sun rises in the evening.*

ZEN SAYING

By Thomas Merton

THE ASIAN JOURNAL
THE COLLECTED POEMS
EIGHTEEN POEMS
GANDHI ON NON-VIOLENCE
THE GEOGRAPHY OF LOGRAIRE
THE LITERARY ESSAYS
MY ARGUMENT WITH THE GESTAPO
NEW SEEDS OF CONTEMPLATION
RAIDS ON THE UNSPEAKABLE
SEEDS OF CONTEMPLATION
SELECTED POEMS
THOMAS MERTON IN ALASKA
THOUGHTS ON THE EAST
THE WAY OF CHUANG TZU
THE WISDOM OF THE DESERT
ZEN AND THE BIRDS OF APPETITE

About Thomas Merton

WORDS AND SILENCE:
ON THE POETRY OF THOMAS MERTON
by Sister Thérèse Lentfoehr

Published by New Directions

# ZEN
# AND THE
# BIRDS OF APPETITE

THOMAS MERTON

A NEW DIRECTIONS BOOK

*For Amiya Chakravarty*

# CONTENTS

# AUTHOR'S NOTE

Where there is carrion lying, meat-eating birds circle and descend. Life and death are two. The living attack the dead, to their own profit. The dead lose nothing by it. They gain too, by being disposed of. Or they seem to, if you must think in terms of gain and loss. Do you then approach the study of Zen with the idea that there is something to be gained by it? This question is not intended as an implicit accusation. But it *is*, nevertheless, a serious question. Where there is a lot of fuss about "spirituality," "enlightenment" or just "turning on," it is often because there are buzzards hovering around a corpse. This hovering, this circling, this descending, this celebration of victory, are not what is meant by the Study of Zen— even though they may be a highly useful exercise in other contexts. And they enrich the birds of appetite.

Zen enriches no one. There is no body to be found. The birds may come and circle for a while in the place where it is thought to be. But they soon go elsewhere. When they are gone, the "nothing," the "no-body" that was there, suddenly appears. That is Zen. It was there all the time but the scavengers missed it, because it was not their kind of prey.

PART ONE

# THE STUDY OF ZEN

*Better to see the face than to hear the name.*

ZEN SAYING

"There is nothing," says Lévi-Strauss, "which can be conceived of or understood short of the basic demands of its structure." He is talking about primitive kinship systems, and of the key role played in them by maternal uncles. And I must admit from the outset that uncles have nothing to do with Zen; nor am I about to prove that they have. But the statement is universal. "There is *nothing* which can be understood short of the basic demands of its structure." This raises a curious question: I wonder if Zen could somehow be fitted into the patterns of a structuralist anthropology? And if so, can it be "understood?" And at once one sees that the question can probably be answered by "yes" and by "no."

In so far as Zen is part of a social and religious complex, in so far as it seems to be related to other elements of a cultural system—"yes." In so far as Zen is Zen *Buddhism,* "yes." But in that case what fits into the system is *Buddhism* rather than *Zen.* The more Zen is considered as *Buddhist* the more it can be grasped as an expression of man's cultural and religious impulse. In that case Zen can be seen as having a special kind of structure with basic demands that are *structural* demands and therefore open to scientific investigation—and the more it can seem to have a definite character to be grasped and "understood."

First published in *Cimarron Review,* (Oklahoma State University), June, 1968.

When Zen is studied in this way, it is seen in the context of Chinese and Japanese history. It is seen as a product of the meeting of speculative Indian Buddhism with practical Chinese Taoism and even Confucianism. It is seen in the light of the culture of the T'ang dynasty, and the teachings of various "houses." It is related to other cultural movements. It is studied in its passage into Japan and its integration into Japanese civilization. And then a great deal of things about Zen come to seem important, even essential. The *Zendo* or meditation hall. The *Zazen* sitting. The study of the *Koan*. The costume. The lotus seat. The bows. The visits to the *Roshi* and the *Roshi's* technique for determining whether one has attained *Kensho* or *Satori,* and helping one to do this.

Zen, seen in this light, can then be set up against other religious structures—for instance that of Catholicism, with its sacraments, its liturgy, its mental prayer (now no longer practised by many), its devotions, its laws, its theology, its Bible; its cathedrals and convents; its priesthood and its hierarchical organization; its Councils and Encyclicals.

One can examine both of them and conclude that they have a few things in common. They share certain cultural and religious features. They are "religions." One is an Asian religion, the other is a Western, Judeo-Christian religion. One offers man a metaphysical enlightenment, the other a theological salvation. Both can be seen as oddities, pleasant survivals of a past which is no more, but which one can nevertheless appreciate just as one appreciates Noh plays, the sculpture of Chartres or the music of Monteverdi. One can further refine one's investigations and imagine (quite wrongly) that because Zen is simple and austere, it has a great deal in common with Cistercian monasticism, which is also austere—or once was. They do share a certain taste for simplicity, and it is possible that the builders of twelfth-century Cistercian churches in Burgundy and Provence were illuminated by a kind of instinctive Zen vision in their work, which does have the luminous poverty and solitude that Zen calls *Wabi*.

Nevertheless, studied as *structures,* as *systems,* and as *religions,* Zen and Catholicism don't mix any better than oil and water. One can assume that from one side and the other, from the *Zendo* and from the university, monastery or curia, persons might convene for polite and informed discussion. But their differences would remain inviolate. They would return to their several structures and bed down again in their own systems, having attained just enough understanding to recognize themselves as utterly alien to one another. All this is true as long as Zen is considered specifically as Zen *Buddhism,* as a school or sect of Buddhism, as forming part of the religious system which we call "the Buddhist Religion."

When we look a little closer however, we find very serious and responsible practitioners of Zen first denying that it is "a religion," then denying that it is a sect or school, and finally denying that it is confined to Buddhism and its "structure." For instance, one of the great Japanese Zen Masters, Dogen, the founder of Soto Zen, said categorically: "Anybody who would regard Zen as a school or sect of Buddhism and call it *Zen-shu,* Zen school, is a devil."

To define Zen in terms of a religious system or structure is in fact to destroy it—or rather to miss it completely, for what cannot be "constructed" cannot be destroyed either. Zen is not something which is grasped by being set within distinct limits or given a characteristic outline or easily recognizable features so that, when we see these distinct and particular forms, we say: "There it is!" Zen is not understood by being set apart in its own category, separated from everything else: "It is *this* and *not that.*" On the contrary, in the words of D.T. Suzuki, Zen is "beyond the world of opposites, a world

3

built up by intellectual distinction . . . a spiritual world of nondistinction which involves achieving an absolute point of view." Yet this too could easily become a trap if we "distinguished" the Absolute from the nonabsolute in a Western, Platonic way. Suzuki therefore immediately adds, "The Absolute is in no way distinct from the world of discrimination. . . . The Absolute is in the world of opposites and not apart from it." (D.T. Suzuki, *The Essence of Buddhism,* London, 1946, p. 9) We see from this that Zen is outside all particular structures and distinct forms, and that it is neither opposed to them nor not-opposed to them. It neither denies them nor affirms them, loves them nor hates them, rejects them nor desires them. Zen is consciousness unstructured by particular form or particular system, a trans-cultural, trans-religious, trans-formed consciousness. It is therefore in a sense "void." But it can shine through this or that system, religious or irreligious, just as light can shine through glass that is blue, or green, or red, or yellow. If Zen has any preference it is for glass that is plain, has no color, and is "just glass."

In other words to regard Zen *merely* and *exclusively* as Zen Buddhism is to falsify it and, no doubt, to betray the fact that one has no understanding of it whatever. Yet this does not mean that there cannot be "Zen Buddhists," but these surely will realize (precisely because they are Zen-men) the difference between their Buddhism and their Zen—even while admitting that for them their Zen is in fact the purest expression of Buddhism. But, of course, the reason for that is that Buddhism itself (more than any "religious system") points beyond any theological or philosophical "ism." It demands *not to be a system* (while at the same time, like other religions, presenting a peculiar temptation to systematizers). The real drive of Buddhism is toward an enlightenment which is precisely a breakthrough into what is beyond system, beyond cultural and social structures, and beyond religious rite and belief (even where it accepts many kinds of systematic religious and cultural superstructures—Tibetan, Burmese, Japanese, etc.).

Now if we reflect a moment, we will realize that in Christianity, too, as well as in Islam, we have various admittedly unusual people who see beyond the "religious" aspect of their faith. Karl Barth for instance—in the pure tradition of Protestantism—protested against calling Christianity "a religion" and vehemently denied that Christian faith could be understood as long as it was seen embedded in social and cultural structures. These structures, he believed, were completely alien to it, and a perversion of it. In Islam, too, the Sufis sought *Fana,* the extinction of that social and cultural self which was determined by the structural forms of religious customs. This extinction is a breakthrough into a realm of mystical liberty in which the "self" is lost and then reconstituted in *Baqa*—something like the "New Man" of Christianity, as understood by the Christian mystics (including the Apostles). "I live," said Paul, "now not I but Christ lives in me."

And in Zen enlightenment, the discovery of the "original face before you were born" is the discovery not that one *sees* Buddha but that one *is* Buddha and that Buddha is not what the images in the temple had led one to expect: for there is no longer any image, and consequently nothing to see, no one to see it, and a Void in which no image is even conceivable. "The true seeing," said Shen Hui, "is when there is no seeing."

What this means then is that Zen is outside all structures and forms. We may use certain externals of Zen Buddhist monasticism—along with the paintings of Zen artists, their poems, their brief and vivid sayings—to help us approach Zen.

5

The peculiar quality of Chinese and Japanese art that is influenced by Zen is that it is able to suggest what cannot be said, and, by using a bare minimum of form, to awaken us to the formless. Zen painting tells us just enough to alert us to what is *not* and is nevertheless "right there." Zen calligraphy, by its peculiar suppleness, dynamism, abandon, contempt for "prettiness" and for formal "style," reveals to us something of the freedom which is not transcendent in some abstract and intellectual sense, but which employs a minimum of form without being attached to it, and is therefore free from it. The Zen consciousness is compared to a mirror. A modern Zen writer says:

> "The mirror is thoroughly egoless and mindless. If a flower comes it reflects a flower, if a bird comes it reflects a bird. It shows a beautiful object as beautiful, an ugly object as ugly. Everything is revealed as it is. There is no discriminating mind or self-consciousness on the part of the mirror. If something comes, the mirror reflects; if it disappears the mirror just lets it disappear . . . no traces of anything are left behind. Such non-attachment, the state of no-mind, or the truly free working of a mirror is compared here to the pure and lucid wisdom of Buddha."
> (Zenkei Shibayma, *On Zazen Wasan*, Kyoto, 1967, p. 28)

What is meant here is that the Zen consciousness does not distinguish and categorize what it sees in terms of social and cultural standards. It does not try to fit things into artificially preconceived structures. It does not judge beauty and ugliness according to canons of taste—even though it may have its own taste. If it seems to judge and distinguish, it does so only enough to point beyond judgment to the pure void. It does not settle down in its judgment as final. It does not erect its judgment into a structure to be defended against all comers.

Here we can fruitfully reflect on the deep meaning of Jesus' saying: "Judge not, and you will not be judged." Be-

6

yond its moral implications, familiar to all, there is a Zen dimension to this word of the Gospel. Only when this Zen dimension is grasped will the moral bearing of it be fully clear!

As to the notion of the "Buddha mind"—it is not something esoteric to be laboriously acquired, something "not-there" which has to be put there (where?) by the assiduous mental and physical pummeling of *Roshis, Koans* and all the rest. "The Buddha is your everyday mind."

The trouble is that as long as you are given to distinguishing, judging, categorizing and classifying—or even contemplating—you are superimposing something else on the pure mirror. You are filtering the light through a system as if convinced that this will improve the light.

Cultural structures and forms are there, no doubt. There is no such thing as getting along without them or treating them as if they did not exist. But there eventually comes a time when like Moses we see that the thornbush of cultural and religious forms is suddenly on fire and we are summoned to approach it without shoes—and probably also without feet. Is the fire other than the Bush? More than the Bush? Or is it more the Bush than the Bush itself? The Burning Bush of Exodus reminds us strangely of the *Prajnaparamita Sutra:* "Form is emptiness, emptiness itself is form; form does not differ from emptiness (the Void), emptiness does not differ from form; whatever is form, that is emptiness, whatever is emptiness, that is form. . . ." So too the words from the flame-and-bush in Exodus: "I am what I am." These words go beyond position and negation, in fact no one quite knows what the Hebrew means. The scholars make their surmises according to the spirit of the age: now essentialist ("Pure - self - subsistent - Being - in - Act"), now existentialist ("I - won't - tell - you - so - mind - your - own - business - which - is - not - to -

know - but - to - do - what - you - will - do - next - time - I - am - around").

In other words, we begin to divine that Zen is not only beyond the formulations of Buddhism but it is also in a certain way "beyond" (and even pointed to by) the revealed message of Christianity. That is to say that when one breaks through the limits of cultural and structural religion—or irreligion— one is liable to end up, by "birth in the Spirit," or just by intellectual awakening, in a simple void where all is liberty because all is the actionless action, called by the Chinese *Wu-wei* and by the New Testament the "freedom of the Sons of God." Not that they are theologically one and the same, but they have at any rate the same kind of limitlessness, the same lack of inhibition, the same psychic fullness of creativity, which mark the fully integrated maturity of the "enlightened self." The "mind of Christ" as described by St. Paul in Philippians 2 may be theologically worlds apart from the "mind of Buddha"—this I am not prepared to discuss. But the utter "self-emptying" of Christ—and the self-emptying which makes the disciple one with Christ in *His* kenosis—can be understood and has been understood in a very Zen-like sense as far as psychology and experience are concerned.

Thus with all due deference to the vast doctrinal differences between Buddhism and Christianity, and preserving intact all respect for the claims of the different religions: in no way mixing up the Christian "vision of God" with Buddhist "enlightenment," we can nevertheless say that the two have this psychic "limitlessness" in common. And they tend to describe it in much the same language. It is now "emptiness," now "dark night," now "perfect freedom," now "no-mind," now "poverty" in the sense used by Eckhart and by D.T. Suzuki later on in this book (see p. 110).

At this point I may take occasion to say clearly that, in my

8

dialog with Dr. Suzuki, my choice of Cassian's "purity of heart" as a Christian expression of Zen-consciousness was an unfortunate example. No doubt there are passages in Cassian and Evagrius Ponticus and other contemplatives of the Egyptian Desert which suggest some tendency toward the "emptiness" of Zen. But Cassian's idea of "purity of heart," with its Platonic implications, while it may or may not be mystical, is not yet Zen because it still maintains that the supreme consciousness resides in a distinct heart which is pure and which is therefore ready and even worthy to receive a vision of God. It is still very aware of a "pure," distinct and separate self-consciousness. A fuller and truer expression of Zen in Christian experience is given by Meister Eckhart. He admits that: "To be a proper abode for God and fit for God to act in, a man should also be free from all things and actions, both inwardly and outwardly." This is Cassian's "purity of heart," and it also corresponds to the idea of "spiritual virginity" in some Christian mystics. But now Eckhart goes on to say that there is much more: *"A man should be so poor that he is not and has not a place for God to act in. To reserve a place would be to maintain distinctions."* "A man should be so disinterested and untrammeled that he does not know what God is doing in him." For, he continues,

> "If it is the case that man is emptied of all things, creatures, himself and god, and *if god could still find a place in him to act* . . . this man is not poor with the most intimate poverty. For God does not intend that man should have a place reserved for him to work in since true poverty of spirit requires that man shall be emptied of god and all his works so that if God wants to act in the soul *he himself must be the place in which he acts.* . . . (God takes then) responsibility for his own action and (is) himself the scene of the action, for God is one who acts within himself." ( R.B. Blakney, *Meister Eckhart, a Modern Translation,* Sermon "Blessed are the Poor," N. Y., 1941, p. 231 )

Because of the peculiar problems this difficult text poses for Christian orthodoxy, the editor of the English version (Blakney) has printed God now with a small g and now with a large one. This is perhaps an unnecessary scruple. In any case this passage reflects Eckhart's Zen-like equation of God as infinite abyss and ground (cf. *Sunyata*), with the true being of the self grounded in Him; hence it is that Eckhart believes: only when there is no self left as a "place" in which God acts, only when God acts purely in Himself, do we at last recover our "true self" (which is in Zen terms "no-self"). "It is here, in this poverty, that man regains the eternal being that once he was, now is and evermore shall be." It is easy to see why those who interpreted this purely in terms of the *theological system* of the time (instead of in terms of the Zen-like experience it was meant to express) found it unacceptable.

Yet the same idea, expressed in slightly different words by Eckhart, is capable of a perfectly orthodox interpretation: Eckhart speaks of "perfect poverty" in which man is even "without God," and "has no place in himself for God to work" (i.e., is beyond purity of heart).

> "Man's last and highest parting occurs when for God's sake he takes leave of god. St. Paul took leave of god for God's sake and gave up all that he might get from god as well as all he might give—together with every idea of god. In parting with these he parted with god for God's sake and God remained in him as God is in his own nature —not as he is conceived by anyone to be—nor yet as something yet to be achieved, but more as an is-ness, as God really is. Then he and God were a unit, that is pure unity. Thus one becomes that real person for whom there can be no suffering, any more than the divine essence can suffer." (Blakney, *Meister Eckhart*, p. 204-5)

In such perfect poverty, says Eckhart, one may still have ideas and experiences, yet one is free of them:

"(I do) not regard them as mine to take or leave in either past or future. . . . I (am) free and empty of them in this now moment, the present. . . ." (Blakney, *Meister Eckhart,* p. 207)

Beyond the thinking, reflecting, willing and loving self, and even beyond the mystical "spark" in the deepest ground of the soul, is the highest agent, "at once pure and free as God is and like him it is a perfect unity." For "there is something in the soul so closely akin to God that is already one with him and need never be united to him." Eckhart goes on to develop this idea of dynamic unity in a marvelous image which is distinctly Western and yet has a deeply Zen-like quality about it. This divine likeness in us which is the core of our being and is "in God" even more than it is "in us," is the focus of God's inexhaustible creative delight.

"In this likeness or identity God takes such delight that he pours his whole nature and being into it. His pleasure is as great, to take a simile, as that of a horse, let loose over a green heath, where the ground is level and smooth, to gallop as a horse will, as fast as he can over the greens-ward—for this is a horse's pleasure and nature. It is so with God. It is his pleasure and rapture to discover identity, because he can always put his whole nature into it—for he is this identity itself." (Blakney, *Meister Eckhart,* p. 205)

From the point of view of logic this poetic development simply does not make sense, but as an expression of inexpressible insight into the very core of life, it is incomparable. It shows, incidentally, how Eckhart understood the Christian doctrine of creation. He admits the separation of the creature and Creator, for this "Something is apart from and strange to all creation." Yet the distinction between Creator and creature does not alter the fact that there is also a basic unity *within ourselves* at the summit of our being where we are "one with God."

If we could identify purely with this summit we would be other than we experience ourselves to be, yet much more truly ourselves than we actually are. So Eckhart says: "If one were wholly this (i.e., this 'Something' or 'unity') he would be both uncreated and unlike any creature. . . . If I should find myself in this essence, even for a moment, I should regard my earthly selfhood as of no more importance than a manure worm." (Blakney, *Meister Eckhart,* p. 205) Yet we must immediately add that it is only in this highest unity that we finally discover the dignity and importance even of our "earthly self" which does not exist apart from it, but in it and by it. The tragedy is that our consciousness is totally alienated from this inmost ground of our identity. And in Christian mystical tradition, this inner split and alienation is the real meaning of "original sin."

This is all very close to the expressions we find everywhere in the Zen Masters. But it is also intended to be purely Christian for, as Eckhart says, it is precisely in this pure poverty when one is no longer a "self" that one recovers one's true identity in God: This true identity is the "birth of Christ in us." Curiously, then, for Eckhart, it is when we lose our special, separate cultural and religious identity—the "self" or "persona" that is the subject of virtues as well as visions, that perfects itself by good works, that advances in the practice of piety—that Christ is finally born in us in the highest sense. (Eckhart does not deny the sacramental teaching of the birth of Christ in us by baptism, but he is interested in something more fully developed.)

Obviously these teachings of Eckhart were found very disturbing. His taste for paradox, his deliberate use of expressions which outraged conventional religious susceptibilities, in order to awaken his hearers to a new dimension of experience, left him open to the attacks of his enemies. Some of his teachings were officially condemned by the Church—and many of these are being reinterpreted today by scholars in a fully orthodox sense. This is not however what concerns us here. Eckhart can best be appreciated for what is really best in him: and this is not something that is to be found within the framework of a theological system but *outside* it. In all that he tried to say, whether in familiar or in startling terms, Eckhart was trying to point to something that cannot be structured and cannot be contained within the limits of any system. He was not trying to construct a new dogmatic theology, but was trying to give expression to the great creative renewal of the mystical consciousness which was sweeping through the Rhineland and the Low Countries in his time. If Eckhart is studied in the framework of a religious and cultural structure, he is undoubtedly intriguing; yet we may entirely miss the point of what he was saying and become involved in side issues. Seen in relation to those Zen Masters on the other side of the earth who, like him, deliberately used extremely paradoxical expressions, we can detect in him the same kind of consciousness as theirs. Whatever Zen may be, however you define it, it is somehow there in Eckhart. But the way to see it is not first to define Zen and then apply the definition both to him and to the Japanese Zen Masters. The real way to study Zen is to penetrate the outer shell and taste the inner kernel which cannot be defined. Then one realizes in oneself the reality which is being talked about.

As Eckhart says:

"The shell must be cracked apart if what is in it is to come out, for if you want the kernel you must break the shell. And therefore if you want to discover nature's nakedness you must destroy its symbols, and the farther you get in the nearer you come to its essence. When you come to the One that gathers all things up into itself, there you must stay." (Blakney, *Meister Eckhart*, p. 148)

A Zen *Mondo* sums it all up perfectly:

A Zen Master said to his disciple: "Go get my rhinoceros-horn fan."
Disciple: "Sorry, Master, it is broken."
Master: "Okay, then get me the rhinoceros."

# THE NEW CONSCIOUSNESS

One would like to open this discussion with a reassuring and simple declaration, to say without ambiguity or hesitation: Christian renewal has meant that Christians are now wide open to Asian religions, ready, in the words of Vatican II, to "acknowledge, preserve and promote the spiritual and moral goods" found among them. It is not that simple.

In some respects, progressive Christians were never *less* disposed to this kind of openness. True, they approve all forms of communication and inter-religious dialogue on principle. But the new, secular, "post-Christian" Christianity, which is activistic, antimystical, social and revolutionary, tends to take for granted a great deal of the Marxist assumptions about religion as the opium of the people. In fact, these movements aspire to a kind of Christian repentance on this point, and seek with the greatest fervor to prove that there is no opium about *us!* But, knowing little or nothing about Asian religions, and associating Asia with opium anyway (conveniently forgetting that it was the West that forced opium into China by means of war!), they are still satisfied with the old clichés about "life-denying Buddhism," "selfish navel-gazing," and *Nirvana* as a sort of drugged trance.

The purpose of the present book is not apologetic; but if it were, I should feel myself obliged to argue in favor of Bud-

Excerpts from the essay, originally titled "The Self of Modern Man and the New Christian Consciousness," first published and copyrighted by the R.M. Bucke Memorial Society's (Montreal) *Newsletter-Review,* Volume II, No. 1, April, 1967.

dhism against these absurd and unexamined prejudices. I might want to suggest, for instance, that a religion which forbids the taking of *any* life without absolute necessity is hardly "life-denying" (see Appendix, p. 93), and to add that it is a little odd that this accusation should be made by people who, some of them invoking the name of Christ, are ravaging a small Asian country with napalm and dynamite, and doing their best to reduce whole areas of the country to a state of lifelessness. But, I repeat, this is not a book of apologetics.

Of course there are many Christians who are very much aware that there is something to be learnt from Hinduism, Buddhism, Confucianism, and especially from Yoga and Zen. Among these are those few Western Jesuits in Japan who have had the courage to practice Zen in Zen monasteries, as well as the Japanese Cistercians who are becoming interested in Zen in their own monasteries. There are also American and European Benedictines who are taking a more than academic interest in Asian religion.

However, there are problems. Both conservative and progressive Christians tend to be suspicious of Asian religion for various reasons. Conservatives because they think all Asian religious thought is pantheistic and incompatible with the Christian belief in God as Creator. Progressives because they think all Asian religions are purely and simply world-denying evasions into trance, and systematic repudiations of matter, the body, the senses and so on, with the eventual result that they are passive, quietistic and stagnant. This is part of the general Western myth about the mysterious Orient which is thought to have long since subsided quietly into psychic death, with no hope of any kind of salvation except from the dynamic, creative, life-affirming, progressive West.

Now it is true that the civilizations of India and China—and of other parts of Asia—found it impossible to cope with

Western colonialism except by resorting to some of the West's own methods. And it is true that the whole world is in the middle of a cultural and social revolution, the most active center of which is now Asia. Finally, the Chinese cultural revolution is itself one of the most radical, most brutal repudiations of the ancient spiritual heritage of Asia. All these well-known facts give added weight to the prevalent Western ideas about "Asian mysticism" being at best a kind of systematic moral and intellectual suicide.

The somewhat disconcerting vogue for exploring Asian religious experience in the West does not convince progressive Christians that there is much to it. Beats, hippies and other such types may gain a kind of grudging respect from Christians as quasi-eschatological sects—but their mystical leanings are not what the progressive Christian admires in them. The influence of Barth and the New Orthodoxy (in Protestantism), together with the Biblical renewal everywhere, is probably still very important in this antimystical bias.

At the same time, it is not easy to generalize. A "Death-of-God" theologian like Altizer is not only well-informed about Buddhism but also seems to have something of an attraction to it.

Hence nothing too definite can be said about the attitude of the new Christian thinkers toward Hinduism, Buddhism, or Zen—the latter being considered perhaps an "extreme" form of Asian world-denial. The generalized attitude of suspiciousness and negation is based on ignorance.

This essay will concern itself less with Zen than with the Christian consciousness itself, and with the new development that makes Christianity today frankly activistic, secular and antimystical. Is this new consciousness really a return to a primitive Christian spirit? How does it differ from the kind of consciousness that remained more or less the same from Augustine to Maritain in Western Catholicism?

It was assumed until quite recently that the experience of the first Christians was still accessible to fervent Christians of our day in all its purity, provided certain conditions were faithfully fulfilled. The consciousness of the modern Christian was thought to be essentially the same as that of the Christian of the Apostolic age. If it differed, it did so only in certain accidentals of culture, due to the expansion of the Church in time and space.

Modern scholarship has thoroughly questioned this assumption. It has raised the problem of a radical discontinuity between the experience of the first Christians and that of later generations. The first Christians experienced themselves as men "of the last days," newly created in Christ as members of his new kingdom, expecting his imminent return: they were men entirely delivered from the "old aeon" and from all its concerns. They experienced a new life of liberation "in the Spirit" and the perfect freedom of men who received all from God as pure gift, in Christ, with no further responsibility to "this world" than to announce the glad tidings of the imminent" reestablishment of all things in Christ." They were, in a word, prepared for entry into the kingdom and the new creation in their own lifetime. "Let grace come," said the *Didache,* and let this world pass away!"

Of course these elements remained present in Christian theology. But the development of a new historical dimension of Christianity radically altered the perspective and consequently also the experience in which these truths of faith were apprehended by Christians as individuals and as a community. With the help of concepts from Hellenic philosophy, these eschatological ideas were given a *metaphysical* dimension. These truths of Christian belief were now experienced "statically" instead of "dynamically," and furthermore, from being intuited metaphysically they also developed into *mystical* experiences.

When it was discovered that the *Parousia* (coming of Christ) was put off into the future, then martyrdom was regarded as the way to enter directly into his kingdom here and now. The experience of martyrdom was in fact, for many of the martyrs, also a mystical experience of union with Christ in his crucifixion and resurrection (see for instance St. Ignatius of Antioch). After the age of the martyrs the ascetics and monks sought union with God in their lives of solitude and self-denial, which they also justified philosophically and theologically by recourse to Hellenic and Oriental ideas. Thus, it is argued, the existential sense of Christian encounter with God in Christ and in the Church as a *happening* (marked by divine freedom and pure gift) became more and more an experience of stabilized *being:* the Christian consciousness was not centered on an event but on the acquisition of a new ontological status and a "new nature." Grace came to be experienced not as God's act but as God's nature shared by "divine sonship" and ultimately in "divinization." This developed eventually into the idea of mystical nuptials with Christ or, in the terms of ontological mysticism (*Wesensmystik*), into absorption in the Godhead through the Word by the action of the Spirit.

There is no space here to develop this critical historical analysis or to evaluate it. What matters is the question it raises: the question of a radical shift in the Christian consciousness, and hence in the Christian's experience of himself in relation to Christ and to the Church. This question is being discussed from many viewpoints in Catholic circles since Vatican II. It is implicit in new explorations of the nature of faith, in new studies of ecclesiology and of Christology, in the new

19

liturgy and everywhere. Conservative Catholics find this questioning of the accepted categories disturbing. Progressives tend to react forcefully against a metaphysical or even mystical consciousness as "un-Christian."

The metaphysical stability of this ancient view, which over the centuries became traditional, was comforting and secure. Moreover it was inseparable from a stable and authoritarian concept of hierarchical Church structure. A return to a more dynamic and charismatic Christianity—claimed to be that of the first Christians—characterized the Protestant attack on these ancient structures, which depended on a static and metaphysical outlook. More radical Catholics realize this today and perhaps take a certain pleasure in using a fluid, elusive terminology calculated to produce a maximum of anxiety and confusion in less adventurous minds. This dynamism questions all that is static and accepted, and it occasionally makes for good newspaper copy, but the results are not always to be taken very seriously. However that may be, the whole question of Christian, especially Catholic, mysticism is affected by it. If mysticism is summarily identified with the "Hellenic" and "Medieval" Christian experience, it is more and more rejected as non-Christian. The new, radical Catholicism tends to make this identification. The Christian is invited to repudiate all aspiration to personal contemplative union with God and to deep mystical experience, because this is an infidelity to the true Christian revelation, a human substitution for God's saving word, a pagan evasion, an individualistic escape from community. By this token also the Christian dialogue with Oriental religions, with Hinduism and especially with Zen, is considered rather suspect, though of course since dialogue is "progressive" one must not attack it openly as such.

It may however be pertinent to remark here that the term "ecumenism" is not held to be applicable to dialogue with non-Christians. There is an essential difference, say these progressive Catholics, between the dialogue of Catholics with other Christians and the dialogue of Catholics with Hindus or Buddhists. While it is assumed that Catholics and Protestants can learn from each other, and that they can progress together toward a new Christian self-understanding, many progressive Catholics would not concede this to dialogue with non-Christians. Once again, the assumption is that since Hinduism and Buddhism are "metaphysical" and "static" or even "mystical" they have ceased to have any relevance in our time. Only the Catholics who are still convinced of the importance of Christian mysticism are also aware that much is to be learned from a study of the techniques and experience of Oriental religions. But these Catholics are regarded at times with suspicion, if not derision, by progressives and conservatives alike.

The question arises: which outlook comes closer to the primitive Christian experience? Is the supposedly "static" and metaphysical outlook really a rupture and a contradiction, violating the purity of the original Christian awareness? Is the "dynamic" and "existential" approach a return to the primitive view? Must we choose between them?

Is the long tradition of Christian mysticism, from the post-Apostolic age, the Alexandrian and Cappadocian Fathers, down to Eckhart, Tauler, the Spanish mystics and the modern mystics, simply a deviation? When people who cannot entrust themselves to the Church as she now is, nevertheless look with interest and sympathy into the writings of the mystics, are they to be reproved by Christians and admonished to seek rather a more limited and more communal experience of fellowship with progressive believers on the latter's terms? Is this the only true way to understand Christian experience? Is there really a problem, and if there is, what precisely is it?

Supposing that the only authentic Christian experience is that of the first Christians, can this be recovered and reconstructed in any way whatever? And if so, is it to be "mystical" or "prophetic"? And in any case, *what is it?* The present notes cannot hope to answer such questions. Their only purpose is to consider the conflict in Christian consciousness today and to make a guess or two that might point toward avenues of further exploration.

First of all, the "Christian consciousness" of modern man can never purely and simply be the consciousness of a first-century inhabitant of the Roman Empire. It is bound to be a modern consciousness.

In our evaluation of the modern consciousness, we have to take into account the still overwhelming importance of the Cartesian *cogito*. Modern man, in so far as he is still Cartesian (he is of course going far beyond Descartes in many respects), is a subject for whom his own self-awareness as a thinking, observing, measuring and estimating "self" is absolutely primary. It is for him the one indubitable "reality," and all truth starts here. The more he is able to develop his consciousness as a subject over against objects, the more he can understand things in their relations to him and one another, the more he can manipulate these objects for his own interests, but also, at the same time, the more he tends to isolate himself in his own subjective prison, to become a detached observer cut off from everything else in a kind of impenetrable alienated and transparent bubble which contains all reality in the form of purely subjective experience. Modern consciousness then tends to create this solipsistic bubble of awareness—an ego-self imprisoned in its own consciousness, isolated and out of touch with other such selves in so far as they are all "things" rather than persons.

It is this kind of consciousness, exacerbated to an extreme, which has made inevitable the so called "death of God." Cartesian thought began with an attempt to reach God as object by starting from the thinking self. But when God becomes object, he sooner or later "dies," because God as object is ultimately unthinkable. God as object is not only a mere abstract concept, but one which contains so many internal contradictions that it becomes entirely nonnegotiable except when it is hardened into an idol that is maintained in existence by a sheer act of will. For a long time man continued to be capable of this willfulness: but now the effort has become exhausting and many Christians have realized it to be futile. Relaxing the effort, they have let go the "God-object" which their fathers and grandfathers still hoped to manipulate for their own ends. Their weariness has accounted for the element of resentment which made this a conscious "murder" of the deity. Liberated from the strain of wilfully maintaining an object-God in existence, the Cartesian consciousness remains none the less imprisoned in itself. Hence the need to break out of itself and to meet "the other" in "encounter," "openness," "fellowship," "communion."

Yet the great problem is that for the Cartesian consciousness the "other," too, is object. There is no need here to retail the all-important modern effort to restore man's awareness of his fellow man to an "I–Thou" status. Is a genuine I–Thou relationship possible *at all* to a purely Cartesian subject?

Meanwhile, let us remind ourselves that another, metaphysical, consciousness is still available to modern man. It starts not from the thinking and self-aware subject but from Being, ontologically seen to be beyond and prior to the subject–object division. Underlying the subjective experience of the individual self there is an immediate experience of Being. This is totally different from an experience of self-consciousness. It is completely nonobjective. It has in it none of the split and alienation that occurs when the subject becomes aware of itself as a quasi-object. The consciousness of Being (whether considered positively or negatively and apophatically as in Buddhism) is an immediate experience that goes beyond reflexive awareness. It is not "consciousness *of*" but *pure consciousness,* in which the subject as such "disappears."

Posterior to this immediate experience of a ground which transcends experience, emerges the subject with its self-awareness. But, as the Oriental religions and Christian mysticism have stressed, this self-aware subject is not final or absolute; it is a provisional self-construction which exists, for practical purposes, only in a sphere of relativity. Its existence has meaning in so far as it does not become fixated or centered upon itself as ultimate, learns to function not as its own center but "from God" and "for others." The Christian term "from God" implies what the nontheistic religious philosophies conceive as a hypothetical Single Center of all beings, what T. S. Eliot called "the still point of the turning world," but which Buddhism for example visualizes not as "point" but as "Void." (And of course the Void is not visualized at all.)

In brief, this form of consciousness assumes a totally different kind of self-awareness from that of the Cartesian thinking-self which is its own justification and its own center. Here the individual is aware of himself as a self-to-be-dissolved in self-giving, in love, in "letting-go," in ecstasy, in God—there are many ways of phrasing it.

The self is not its own center and does not orbit around itself; it is centered on God, the one center of all, which is "everywhere and nowhere," in whom all are encountered, from whom all proceed. Thus from the very start this consciousness is disposed to encounter "the other" with whom it is already united anyway "in God."

The metaphysical intuition of Being is an intuition of a

*ground of openness,* indeed of a kind of ontological openness and an infinite generosity which communicates itself to everything that is. "The good is diffusive of itself," or "God is love." Openness is not something to be acquired, but a radical gift that has been lost and must be recovered (though it is still in principle "there" in the roots of our created being). This is more or less metaphysical language, but there is also a non-metaphysical way of stating this. It does not consider God either as Immanent or as Transcendent but as grace and presence, hence neither as a "Center" imagined somewhere "out there" nor "within ourselves." It encounters him not as Being but as Freedom and Love. I would say from the outset that the important thing is not to *oppose* this gracious and prophetic concept to the metaphysical and mystical idea of union with God, but to show where the two ideas really seek to express the same kind of consciousness or at least to approach it, in varying ways.

\*     \*     \*     \*

The French Marxist Roger Garaudy has said that the religious experience of a St. Theresa is something that he finds interesting and worth studying in Christianity. This has perhaps embarrassed some of those Christians most concerned with dialogue with Marxists. There is no question that the Christian mystics, though repudiated by some Christians, remain mysterious signs and challenges to those who, though they remain outside the Church and are confirmed "unbelievers," nevertheless still seek a deeper dimension of consciousness than that of a horizontal movement across the surface of life—what Max Picard called "the flight" (from God). They are attracted by the mystical consciousness but repelled equally by the triumphalist institution of the Church and by the activist and aggressive noisiness of some progressives.

St. Theresa is a classic example of Christian experience. Though a mystic with her own special charisma, it has long been taken for granted, at least by traditional Catholics, that her mystical consciousness made her actually *aware* of realities which are common to but hidden from all Christians. What others *believed,* she *experienced* in herself.

The mystical consciousness of St. Theresa implies a certain basic attitude toward the self. The thinking and feeling and willing self is not the starting point of all verifiable reality and of all experience. The primal truth, the ground of all being and truth, is in God the Creator of all that is. The starting point of all Christian belief and experience (in this context) is the primal reality of God as Pure Actuality. The "existence of God" is not something seen as deducible from our conscious awareness of our own existence. On the contrary, the experience of the classic Christian mystics is rooted in a metaphysic of being, in which God is intuited as "He Who Is," as the supreme reality, pure Being. The self-centered awareness of the ego is of course a pragmatic psychological reality, but once there has been an inner illumination of pure reality, an awareness of the Divine, the empirical self is seen by comparison to be "nothing," that is to say contingent, evanescent, relatively unreal, real only in relation to its source and end in God, considered not as object but as free ontological source of one's own existence and subjectivity. To understand this attitude, we have to remember that in this view of things Being is not an abstract objective idea but a fundamental concrete intuition directly apprehended in a personal experience that is incontrovertible and inexpressible.

\* \* \* \*

The new Christian consciousness, which tends to reject the Being of God as irrelevant (or even to accept as perfectly obvious the "death of God"), must be seen to be an entirely different matter. Here there is no metaphysical intuition of Being, and hence "being" is reduced to an abstract concept, a cipher to figure with, a purely logical entity, surely nothing to be concretely *experienced*. What is experienced as primary is not "being" or "isness" but individual *consciousness*, reflexive ego-awareness.

This distinction is very important indeed, because if the primary datum of experience and the ultimate test of all truth is simply the self-awareness of the conscious subject, verifying what is obvious to its own consciousness, then that self-awareness would seem to block off and inhibit any real intuition of being. By the nature of the case, being, in this new situation, presents itself not as an immediate datum of intuitive consciousness but as an object of empirical observation—which, as a matter of fact, it cannot possibly be. This has many important consequences. For such a consciousness, a nonobjective metaphysical or mystical intuition becomes, in practice, incomprehensible. The very notion of Being is nonviable, irrelevant and even absurd.

For example, when the mystic (of the classic type) claims to rest absorbed in a simple intuition of God's presence and love without "seeing" or "understanding" any object, the reflexive consciousness (which I am for the sake of convenience calling Cartesian) interprets this in a peculiar way: either as a stubborn fixation on an imaginary object, on "something out there," or as narcissistic repose of the consciousness in itself. It is true that false mysticism can take on some such appearance as this. The only solution to this problem is to admit that quite probably there is no way for this "Cartesian" type of consciousness to really grasp what the mystics of the classic type are talking about. (Hence the astonishing jumble of the authentic and inauthentic in a book like James' *Varieties* of *Religious Experience*.) The same is probably true of the phenomenological consciousness. For either of these, an altogether different road to personal and Christian fulfillment must be found.

The new consciousness naturally turns outward to history, to event, to movement, to progress, and seeks its own identity and fulfilment in action toward historic political or critical goods. In proportion as it is also Biblical and eschatological it approaches the primitive Christian consciousness. But we can see already that "Biblical" and "eschatological" thinking do not comfortably accord with this particular kind of consciousness, and there are already signs that it will soon have to declare itself completely post-Biblical, as well as post-Christian.

Meanwhile drugs have appeared as a *deus ex machina* to enable the self-aware Cartesian consciousness to extend its awareness of itself while seemingly getting out of itself. In other words, drugs have provided the self-conscious self with a substitute for metaphysical and mystical self-transcendence. Perhaps also with a substitute for love? I don't know.

At any rate, the new Christian consciousness would seem to be the product of a kind of phenomenology which more and more questions and repudiates anything that seems to it to be "metaphysical," "Hellenic" and above "mystical." It concerns itself less and less with God as present in being (in his creation) and more and more with God's word as summons to action. God is present not as the experienced transcendent presence which is "wholly other" and reduces everything else to insignificance, but in an inscrutable word summoning to community with other men. But what community, and what other men? The Church in its traditional authoritarian structures is severely criticized—which is not necessarily a bad thing! But the rather more fluid idea of community which "happens" when people are brought together by God's word may perhaps remain very vague and subjective itself. In theory it is excitingly charismatic; in practice it is sometimes strangely capricious. It may conceivably degenerate into mere conviviality or the temporary agreement of political partisans or the mild confabulation of clerical hippies.

Obviously this is not the place to examine a new and completely fluid conception which has not yet taken definite shape. But this much can be said: the developing Christian consciousness is one which is activistic, antimystical, antimetaphysical, which eschews well-defined and concrete forms, and which tends to identify itself with active, progressive, even revolutionary, movements that are on the way but that have not yet reached any kind of clear definition.

In this context, then, the concept of the self as a very present, very concrete center of decision has considerable importance. It matters very much what you are thinking, saying, doing, deciding, here and now. It matters very much what your current commitments are, whom you are with, whom you are against, where you claim to be going, what button you wear, whom you vote for—all this is important. This is obviously proper to men of action who feel that there are old structures to be torn down and new ones to be built. But from such men we must not yet expect either patience with or understanding of mysticism. They will be foredoomed, by their very type of consciousness, to reject it as irrelevant and even un-Christian. Meanwhile we may wonder if what they are developing is not simply a new, more fluid, less doctrinal kind of conformism!

On the other hand, there must be a better reply to them than the mere reaffirmation of the ancient static and classic positions. It is quite possible that the language and metaphysical assumptions of the classic view are out of reach of many modern men. It is quite plausible to assert that the old Hellenic categories are indeed worn out, and that Platonizing thought, even revivified with shots in the arm from Yoga and Zen, will not quite serve in the modern world. What then? Is there some new possibility, some other opening for the Christian consciousness today?

If there is, it will doubtless have to meet the following great needs of man:

*First;* His need for community, for a genuine relationship of authentic love with his fellow man. This will also imply a deep, in fact completely radical, seriousness in approaching those critical problems which threaten man's very survival as a species on earth—war, racial conflict, hunger, economic and political injustice, etc. It is true that the ancient and classic positions—with their counterparts in the East—have too often favored a kind of quietist indifference to these problems.

*Second;* Man's need for an adequate understanding of his everyday self in his ordinary life. There is no longer any place for the kind of idealistic philosophy that removes all reality into the celestial realms and makes temporal existence meaningless. The old metaphysical outlook did not in fact do this—but in proportion as it was *idealistic* it did tend to misconstrue and depreciate the concrete. Man needs to find ultimate sense here and now in the ordinary humble tasks and human problems of every day.

*Third;* Man's need for a whole and integral experience of his own self on all its levels, bodily as well as imaginative, emotional, intellectual, spiritual. There is no place for the cultivation of *one part* of human consciousness, *one aspect* of human experience, at the expense of the others, even on the pretext that what is cultivated is sacred and all the rest profane. A false and divisive "sacredness" or "supernaturalism" can only cripple man.

Let us remember that the modern consciousness deals more and more with *signs* rather than with *things,* let alone persons. The reason for this is that signs are necessary to simplify the overcrowding of the consciousness with objects. The plain facts of modern life make this unavoidable. But it is also very crippling and divisive.

But it is wrong to assume that these great needs demand the hypertrophy of self-consciousness and the elephantiasis of self-will, without which modern man tends to doubt his own reality. On the contrary, I might suggest a *fourth* need of modern man which is precisely liberation from his inordinate self-consciousness, his monumental self-awareness, his obsession with self-affirmation, so that he may enjoy the freedom from concern that goes with being simply what he is and accepting things as they are in order to work with them as he can.

For all these needs, but especially the last, the Christian will do well to return to the simple lessons of the Gospel and understand them, if he can, not in terms of an imminent second coming, but certainly in terms of a new and liberated creation "in the Spirit." Then he can be delivered from the obsessions of a culture that thrives on the stimulation and exploitation of egocentric desire.

But he will also do well, perhaps, to turn to Asian religion and acquire a more accurate understanding of its "unworldliness." Is the basic teaching of Buddhism—on ignorance, deliverance and enlightenment—really life-denying, or is it rather the same kind of life-affirming liberation that we find in the Good News of Redemption, the Gift of the Spirit, and the New Creation?

The following essays will not attempt to develop a systematic thesis on this point, but they will focus on various aspects of Zen, always from a Western and Christian viewpoint, but also with the belief that neither Zen nor Buddhism can really be held to be totally alien to that viewpoint. On the contrary, I believe that Zen has much to say not only to a Christian but also to a modern man. It is nondoctrinal, concrete, direct, existential, and seeks above all to come to grips with life itself, not with ideas about life, still less with party platforms in politics, religion, science or anything else.

# A CHRISTIAN LOOKS AT ZEN

Dr. John C.H. Wu is in a uniquely favorable position to interpret Zen for the West. He has given courses on Zen in Chinese and in American universities. An eminent jurist and diplomat, a Chinese convert to Catholicism, a scholar but also a man of profoundly humorous simplicity and spiritual freedom, he is able to write of Buddhism not from hearsay or study alone, but from within. Dr. Wu is not afraid to admit that he brought Zen, Taoism and Confucianism with him into Christianity. In fact in his well-known Chinese translation of the New Testament he opens the Gospel of St. John with the words, "In the beginning was the Tao."

He nowhere feels himself obliged to pretend that Zen causes him to have dizzy spells or palpitations of the heart. Nor does he attempt the complex and frustrating task of trying to conciliate Zen insights with Christian doctrine. He simply takes hold of Zen and presents it without comment. Anyone who has any familiarity with Zen will immediately admit that this is the only way to talk about it. To approach the subject with an intellectual or theological chip on the shoulder would end only in confusion. The truth of the matter is that you can hardly set Christianity and Zen side by side and compare them. This would almost be like trying to compare mathematics and tennis. And if you are writing a book on tennis which might conceivably be read by many mathematicians, there is little point in bringing mathematics into

First published as preface to John C.H. Wu's *The Golden Age of Zen,* Committee on Compilation of the Chinese Library.

the discussion—best to stick to the tennis. That is what Dr. Wu has done with Zen.

On the other hand, Zen is deliberately cryptic and disconcerting. It seems to say the most outrageous things about the life of the spirit. It seems to jolt even the Buddhist mind out of its familiar thought routines and devout imaginings, and no doubt it will be even more shocking to those whose religious outlook is remote from Buddhism. Zen can sound, at times, frankly and avowedly irreligious. And it is, in the sense that it makes a direct attack on formalism and myth, and regards conventional religiosity as a hindrance to mature spiritual development. On the other hand, in what sense is Zen, as such, "religious" at all? Yet where do we ever find "pure Zen" dissociated from a religious and cultural matrix of some sort? Some of the Zen Masters were iconoclasts. But the life of an ordinary Zen temple is full of Buddhist piety and ritual, and some Zen literature abounds in devotionalism and in conventional Buddhist religious concepts. The Zen of D.T. Suzuki is completely free from all this. But can it be called "typical?" One of the advantages of Dr. Wu's Christian treatment is that he, too, is able to see Zen apart from this accidental setting. It is like seeing the mystical doctrine of St. John of the Cross apart from the somewhat irrelevant backdrop of Spanish baroque. However, the whole study of Zen can bristle with questions like these, and when the well-meaning inquirer receives answers to his questions, then hundreds of other questions arise to take the place of the two or three that have been "answered."

Though much has been said, written and published in the West about Zen, the general reader is probably not much the wiser for most of it. And unless he has some idea of what Zen is all about he may be mystified by Dr. Wu's book, which is full of the classic Zen material: curious anecdotes, strange happenings, cryptic declarations, explosions of illogical humor, not to mention contradictions, inconsistencies, eccentric and even absurd behavior, and all for what? For some apparently esoteric purpose which is never made clear to the satisfaction of the logical Western mind.

Now the reader with a Judeo-Christian background of some sort (and who in the West does not still have some such background?) will naturally be predisposed to misinterpret Zen because he will instinctively take up the position of one who is confronting a "rival system of thought" or a "competing ideology" or an "alien world view" or more simply "a false religion." Anyone who adopts such a position makes it impossible for himself to see what Zen is, because he assumes in advance that it must be something that it expressly refuses to be. Zen is not a systematic explanation of life, it is not an ideology, it is not a world view, it is not a theology of revelation and salvation, it is not a mystique, it is not a way of ascetic perfection, it is not mysticism as this is understood in the West, in fact it fits no convenient category of ours. Hence all our attempts to tag it and dispose of it with labels like "pantheism," "quietism," "illuminism," "Pelagianism," must be completely incongruous, and proceed from a naive assumption that Zen pretends to justify the ways of God to man and to do so falsely. Zen is not concerned with God in the way Christianity is, though one is entitled to discover sophisticated analogies between the Zen experience of the Void (*Sunyata*) and the experience of God in the "unknowing" of apophatic Christian mysticism. However, Zen cannot be properly judged as a mere doctrine, for though there are in it implicit doctrinal elements, they are entirely secondary to the inexpressible Zen experience.

True, we cannot really understand Chinese Zen if we do not grasp the implicit Buddhist metaphysic which it so to speak acts out. But the Buddhist metaphysic itself is hardly doctrinal in our elaborate philosophical and theological sense: Buddhist philosophy is an interpretation of ordinary human experience, but an interpretation which is not revealed by God nor discovered in the access of inspiration nor seen in a mystical light. Basically, Buddhist metaphysics is a very simple and natural elaboration of the implications of Buddha's own experience of enlightenment. Buddhism does not seek primarily to understand or to "believe in" the enlightenment of Buddha as the solution to all human problems, but seeks an existential and empirical participation in that enlightenment experience. It is conceivable that one might have the "enlightenment" without being aware of any discursive philosophical implications at all. These implications are not seen as having any theological bearing whatever, and they point only to the ordinary natural condition of man. It is true that they arrive at certain fundamental deductions which were in the course of time elaborated into complex religious and philosophical systems. But the chief characteristic of Zen is that it rejects all these systematic elaborations in order to get back, as far as possible, to the pure unarticulated and unexplained ground of direct experience. The direct experience of what? Life itself. What it means that I exist, that I live: who is this "I" that exists and lives? What is the difference between an authentic and an illusory awareness of the self that exists and lives? What are and are not the basic facts of existence?

When we in the West speak of "basic facts of existence" we tend immediately to conceive these facts as reducible to certain austere and foolproof propositions—logical statements that are guaranteed to have meaning because they are empirically verifiable. These are what Bertrand Russell called "atomic facts." Now for Zen it is inconceivable that the basic facts of existence should be able to be stated in any proposition however atomic. For Zen, from the moment fact is transferred to a statement it is falsified. One ceases to grasp the naked reality of experience and one grasps a form of words instead. The *verification* that Zen seeks is not to be found in a dialectical transaction involving the reduction of fact to logical statement and the reflective verification of statement by fact. It may be said that long before Bertrand Russell spoke of "atomic facts" Zen had split the atom and made its own kind of statement in the explosion of logic into *Satori* (enlightenment). The whole aim of Zen is not to make foolproof statements about experience, but to come to direct grips with reality without the mediation of logical verbalizing.

But *what* reality? There is certainly a kind of living and nonverbal dialectic in Zen between the ordinary everyday experience of the senses (which is by no means arbitrarily repudiated) and the experience of enlightenment. Zen is not an idealistic rejection of sense and matter in order to ascend to a supposedly invisible reality which alone is real. The Zen experience is a direct grasp of the *unity* of the invisible and the visible, the noumenal and the phenomenal, or, if you prefer, an experiential realization that any such division is bound to be pure imagination.

D.T. Suzuki says: "Tasting, seeing, experiencing, living—all these demonstrate that there is something common to enlightenment-experience and our sense-experience; the one takes place in our innermost being, the other on the periphery of our consciousness. Personal experience thus seems to be the foundation of Buddhist philosophy. In this sense Buddhism is radical empiricism or experientialism, whatever dialectic later developed to probe the meaning of the enlightenment experience." (D.T. Suzuki, *Mysticism: Christian and Buddhist,* N. Y., 1957, p. 48)

Now the great obstacle to mutual understanding between

Christianity and Buddhism lies in the Western tendency to focus not on the Buddhist *experience,* which is essential, but on the *explanation,* which is accidental and which indeed Zen often regards as completely trivial and even misleading.

Buddhist meditation, but above all that of Zen, seeks not to *explain* but to *pay attention,* to *become aware,* to *be mindful,* in other words to develop a certain *kind of consciousness that is above and beyond deception* by verbal formulas—or by emotional excitement. Deception in what? Deception in its grasp of itself as it really is. Deception due to diversion and distraction from what is right there—consciousness itself.

Zen, then, aims at a kind of certainty: but it is not the logical certainty of philosophical proof, still less the religious certainty that comes with the acceptance of the word of God by the obedience of faith. It is rather the certainty that goes with an authentic metaphysical intuition which is also existential and empirical. The purpose of all Buddhism is to refine the consciousness until this kind of insight is attained, and the religious implications of the insight are then variously worked out and applied to life in the different Buddhist traditions.

In the *Mahayana* tradition, which includes Zen, the chief implication of this insight into the human condition is *Karuna* or compassion, which leads to a paradoxical reversal of what the insight itself might seem to imply. Instead of rejoicing in his escape from the phenomenal world of suffering, the Bodhisattva elects to remain in it and finds in it his *Nirvana,* by reason not only of the metaphysic which identifies the phenomenal and the noumenal, but also of the compassionate love which identifies all the sufferers in the round of birth and death with the Buddha, whose enlightenment they potentially share. Though there are a heaven and a hell for Buddhists, these are not ultimate, and in fact it would be entirely ambiguous to assume that Buddha is regarded as a Savior who leads his faithful disciples to *Nirvana* as to a kind of negative heaven. (Pure Land Buddhism or Amidism is, however, distinctly a salvation religion.)

It cannot be repeated too often: in understanding Buddhism it would be a great mistake to concentrate on the "doctrine," the formulated philosophy of life, and to neglect the experience, which is absolutely essential, the very heart of Buddhism. This is in a sense the exact opposite of the situation in Christianity. For Christianity begins with revelation. Though it would be misleading to classify this revelation simply as a "doctrine" and an "explanation" (it is far more than that—the revelation of God Himself in the mystery of Christ) it is nevertheless communicated to us in words, in statements, and everything depends on the believer's accepting the truth of these statements.

Therefore Christianity has always been profoundly concerned with these statements: with the accuracy of their transmission from the original sources, with the precise understanding of their exact meaning, with the elimination and indeed the condemnation of false interpretations. At times this concern has been exaggerated almost to the point of an obsession, accompanied by arbitrary and fanatical insistence on hairsplitting distinctions and the purest niceties of theological detail.

This obsession with doctrinal formulas, juridical order and ritual exactitude has often made people forget that the heart of Catholicism, too, is a *living experience* of unity in Christ which far transcends all conceptual formulations. What too often has been overlooked, in consequence, is that Catholicism is the taste and experience of eternal life: "We announce to you the eternal life which was with the Father and has appeared to us. What we have seen and have heard we announce to you, in order that you also may have fellowship with us and that our fellowship may be with the Father and with His Son Jesus Christ." (I John 1:2-3) Too often the Catholic has imagined himself obliged to stop short at a mere correct and external belief expressed in good moral behavior, instead of entering fully into the life of hope and love consummated by union with the invisible God "in Christ and in the Spirit," thus fully sharing in the Divine Nature. (Ephesians 2:18, 2 Peter 1:4, Col. 1:9-17, I John 4:12-12)

The Second Vatican Council has (we hope) happily put an end to this obsessive tendency in Catholic theological investigation. But the fact remains that for Christianity, a religion of the Word, the understanding of the statements which embody God's revelation of Himself remains a primary concern. Christian experience is a fruit of this understanding, a development of it, a deepening of it.

At the same time, Christian experience itself will be profoundly affected by the idea of revelation that the Christian himself will entertain. For example, if revelation is regarded simply as a system of truths *about* God and an explanation of how the universe came into existence, what will eventually happen to it, what is the purpose of Christian life, what are its moral norms, what will be the rewards of the virtuous, and so on, then Christianity is in effect reduced to a world view, at times a religious philosophy and little more, sustained by a more or less elaborate cult, by a moral discipline and a strict code of Law. "Experience" of the inner meaning of Christian revelation will necessarily be distorted and diminished in such a theological setting. What will such experience be? Not so much a living theological experience of the presence of God in the world and in mankind through the mystery of Christ, but rather a sense of security in one's own correctness: a feeling of confidence that one has been saved, a confidence which is based on the reflex awareness that one holds the correct view of the creation and purpose of the world and that one's behavior is of a kind to be rewarded in the next life. Or, perhaps, since few can attain this level of self-assurance, then the Christian experience becomes one of anxious hope—a struggle with occasional doubt of the "right answers," a painful and constant effort to meet the severe demands of morality and law, and a somewhat desperate recourse to the sacraments which are there to help the weak who must constantly fall and rise again.

This of course is a sadly deficient account of true Christian experience, based on a distortion of the true import of Christian revelation. Yet it is the impression non-Christians often get of Christianity from the outside, and when one proceeds to compare, say, Zen experience in its purity with this diminished and distorted type of "Christian experience," then one's comparison is just as meaningless and misleading as a comparison of Christian philosophy and theology on their highest and most sophisticated level with the myths of a popular and decadent Buddhism.

When we set Christianity and Buddhism side by side, we must try to find the points where a genuinely common ground between the two exists. At the present moment, this is no easy task. In fact it is still practically impossible, as suggested above, to really find any such common ground except in a very schematic and artificial way. After all, what do we mean by Christianity, and what do we mean by Buddhism? Is Christianity Christian Theology? Ethics? Mysticism? Worship? Is our idea of Christianity to be taken without further qualification as the Roman Catholic Church? Or does it include Protestant Christianity? The Protestantism of Luther or that of Bonhoeffer? The Protestantism of the God-is-dead school? The Catholicism of St. Thomas? Of St. Augustine and the Western Church Fathers? A supposedly "pure" Christianity of the Gospels? A demythologized Christianity? A "social Gospel"? And what do we mean by Buddhism? The Theravada Buddhism of Ceylon, or that of Burma? Tibetan Buddhism? Tantric Buddhism? Pure Land Buddhism? Speculative and scholastic Indian Buddhism of the middle ages? Or Zen?

The immense variety of forms taken by thought, experience, worship, moral practice, in both Buddhism and Christianity make all comparisons haphazard, and in the end, when someone like the late Dr. Suzuki announced a study on *Mysticism: Christian and Buddhist,* it turned out to be, rather practically in fact, a comparison between Meister Eckhart and Zen. To narrow the field in this way is at least relevant, though to take Meister Eckhart as representative of Christian mysticism is hazardous. At the same time we must remark that Dr. Suzuki was much too convinced that Eckhart was unusual in his time, and that his statements must have shocked most of his contemporaries. Eckhart's condemnation was in fact due in some measure to rivalry between Dominicans and Franciscans, and his teaching, bold and in some points unable to avoid condemnation, was nevertheless based on St. Thomas to a great extent and belonged to a mystical tradition that was very much alive and was, in fact, the most vital religious force in the Catholicism of his time. Yet to identify Christianity with Eckhart would be completely misleading. That was not what Suzuki intended. He was not comparing the *mystical theology* of Eckhart with the Buddhist philosophy of the Zen Masters, but the *experience* of Eckhart, ontologically and psychologically, with the *experience* of the Zen Masters. This is a reasonable enterprise, offering some small hope of interesting and valid results.

But can one distill from religious or mystical experience

certain pure elements which are common everywhere in all religions? Or is the basic understanding of the nature and meaning of experience so determined by the variety of doctrines that a comparison of experiences involves us inevitably in a comparison of metaphysical or religious beliefs? This is no easy question either. If a Christian mystic has an experience which can be phenomenologically compared with a Zen experience, does it matter that the Christian in fact believes he is personally united with God and the Zen-man interprets his experience as *Sunyata* or the Void being aware of itself? In what sense can these two experiences be called "mystical"? Suppose that the Zen Masters forcefully repudiate any attempt on the part of Christians to grace them with the titles of "mystics"?

It must certainly be said that a certain type of concordist thought today too easily assumes as a basic dogma that "the mystics" in all religions are all experiencing the same thing and are all alike in their liberation from the various doctrines and explanations and creeds of their less fortunate co-religionists. All religions thus "meet at the top," and their various theologies and philosophies become irrelevant when we see that they were merely means for arriving at the same end, and all means are alike efficacious. This has never been demonstrated with any kind of rigor, and though it has been persuasively advanced by talented and experienced minds, we must say that a great deal of study and investigation must be done before much can be said on this very complex question which, once again, seems to imply a purely formalistic view of theological and philosophical doctrines, as if a fundamental belief were something that a mystic could throw off like a suit of clothes and as if his very experience itself were not in some sense modified by the fact that he held this belief.

At the same time, since the personal experience of the

mystic remains inaccessible to us and can only be evaluated indirectly through texts and other testimonials—perhaps written and given by others—it is never easy to say with any security that what a Christian mystic and a Sufi and a Zen Master experience is really "the same thing." What does such a claim really mean? Can it be made at all, without implying (quite falsely) that these higher experiences are "experiences of something"? It therefore remains a very serious problem to distinguish in all these higher forms of religious and metaphysical consciousness what is "pure experience" and what is to some extent determined by language, symbol, or indeed by the "grace of a sacrament." We have hardly reached the point where we know enough about these different states of consciousness and about their metaphysical implications to compare them in accurate detail. But there are nevertheless certain analogies and correspondence which are evident even now, and which may perhaps point out the way to a better mutual understanding. Let us not rashly take them as "proofs" but only as significant clues.

Is it therefore possible to say that both Christians and Buddhists can equally well practice Zen? Yes, if by Zen we mean precisely the quest for direct and pure experience on a metaphysical level, liberated from verbal formulas and linguistic preconceptions. On the theological level the question becomes more complex. It will be touched on at the end of this essay.

The best we can say is that in certain religions, Buddhism for instance, the philosophical or religious framework is of a kind that *can* more easily be discarded, because it has in itself a built-in "ejector," so to speak, by which the meditator is at a certain point flung out from the conceptual apparatus into the Void. It is possible for a Zen Master to say nonchalantly to his disciple, "If you meet the Buddha, kill him!" But in

Christian mysticism the question whether or not the mystic can get along without the human "form" (*Gestalt*) or the sacred Humanity of Christ is still hotly debated, with the majority opinion definitely maintaining the necessity for the Christ of faith to be present as ikon at the center of Christian contemplation. Here again, the question is confused by the failure to distinguish between the objective theology of Christian experience and the actual psychological facts of Christian mysticism in certain cases. And then one must ask, at what point do the abstract demands of theory take precedence over the psychological facts of experience? Or, to what extent does the theology of a theologian without experience claim to interpret correctly the "experienced theology" of the mystic who is perhaps not able to articulate the meaning of his experience in a satisfactory way?

We keep returning to one central question in two forms: the relation of objective doctrine to subjective mystic (or metaphysical) experience, and the difference in this relationship between Christianity and Zen. In Christianity the objective doctrine retains priority both in time and in eminence. In Zen the experience is always prior, not in time but in importance. This is because Christianity is based on supernatural revelation, and Zen, discarding all idea of any revelation and even taking a very independent view of sacred tradition (at least written), seeks to penetrate the natural ontological ground of being. Christianity is a religion of grace and divine gift, hence of total dependence on God. Zen is not easily classified as "a religion" (it is in fact easily separable from any religious matrix and can supposedly flourish in the soil either of non-Buddhist religions or no religion at all), and in any event it strives, like all Buddhism, to make man completely free and independent even in his striving for salvation and enlightenment. Independent of what? Of merely external supports and authorities which keep him from having access to and making use of the deep resources in his own nature and psyche. (Note that Chinese and Japanese Zen both in fact flourished in extremely disciplined and authoritarian cultures. Hence their emphasis on "autonomy" meant in fact an ultimate and humble discovery of inner freedom after one had exhausted all the possibilities of an intensely strict and austere authoritarian training—as the methods of the Zen Masters make abundantly clear!)

On the other hand, let us repeat that we must not neglect the great importance of experience in Christianity. But Christian experience always has a special modality, due to the fact that it is inseparable from the mystery of Christ and the collective life of the Church, the Body of Christ. To experience the mystery of Christ mystically or otherwise is always to transcend the merely individual psychological level and to "experience theologically with the Church" (*sentire cum Ecclesia*). In other words, this experience must always be in some way reducible to a theological form that can be shared by the rest of the Church or that shows that it is a sharing of what the rest of the Church experiences. There is therefore in the recording of Christian experiences a natural tendency to set them down in language and symbols that are easily accessible to other Christians. This may perhaps sometimes mean an unconscious translation of the inexpressible into familiar symbols that are always at hand ready for immediate use.

Zen on the other hand resolutely resists any temptation to be easily communicable, and a great deal of the paradox and violence of Zen teaching and practice is aimed at blasting the foundation of ready explanation and comforting symbol out from under the disciple's supposed "experience." The Christian experience is acceptable in so far as it accords with an established theological and symbolic pattern. The Zen experience is only acceptable on the basis of its absolute singularity, and yet it must be in some way communicable. How?

We cannot begin to understand how the Zen experience is manifested and communicated between master and disciple unless we realize *what* is communicated. If we do not know *what* is supposed to be signified, the strange method of signification will leave us totally disconcerted and more in the dark than we were when we started. Now in Zen, what is communicated is not a message. It is not simply a "word," even though it might be the "word of the Lord." It is not a "what." It does not bring "news" which the receiver did not already have, about something the one informed did not yet know. What Zen communicates is an awareness that is potentially already there but is not conscious of itself. Zen is then not Kerygma but realization, not revelation but consciousness, not news from the Father who sends His Son into this world, but awareness of the ontological ground of our own being here and now, right in the midst of the world. We will see later that the supernatural Kerygma and the metaphysical intuition of the ground of being are far from being incompatible. One may be said to prepare the way for the other. They can well complement each other, and for this reason Zen is perfectly compatible with Christian belief and indeed with Christian mysticism (if we understand Zen in its pure state, as metaphysical intuition).

If this is true, then we must admit it is perfectly logical to admit, with the Zen Masters, that "Zen teaches nothing." One of the greatest of the Chinese Zen Masters, the Patriarch, Hui Neng (7th century A.D.), was asked a leading question by a disciple: "Who has inherited the spirit of the Fifth Patriarch?" (i.e., who is Patriarch now?)

Hui Neng replied: "One who understands Buddhism."

The monk pressed his point: "Have you then inherited it?"

Hui Neng said: "No."

"Why not?" asked the monk.

"Because I do not understand Buddhism."

This story is meant precisely to illustrate the fact that Hui Neng *had* inherited the role of Patriarch, or the charism of teaching the purest Zen. He was qualified to transmit the enlightenment of the Buddha himself to disciples. If he had laid claim to an authoritative teaching that made this enlightenment understandable to those who did not possess it, then he would have been teaching *something else,* that is to say a doctrine *about* enlightenment. He would be disseminating the message of his own understanding of Zen, and in that case he would not be awakening others to Zen in themselves, but imposing on them the imprint of his own understanding and teaching. Zen does not tolerate this kind of thing, since this would be incompatible with the true purpose of Zen: awakening a deep ontological awareness, a wisdom-intuition (*Prajna*) in the ground of the being of the one awakened. And in fact, the pure consciousnes of *Prajna* would not be pure and immediate if it were a consciousness that one understands *Prajna.*

The language used by Zen is therefore in some sense an antilanguage, and the "logic" of Zen is a radical reversal of philosophical logic. The human dilemma of communication is that we cannot communicate ordinarily without words and signs, but even ordinary experience tends to be falsified by our habits of verbalization and rationalization. The convenient tools of language enable us to decide beforehand what we think things mean, and tempt us all too easily to see things only in a way that fits our logical preconceptions and our verbal formulas. Instead of seeing *things* and *facts* as they are we see them as reflections and verifications of the sentences we have previously made up in our minds. We quickly forget how to simply *see* things and substitute our words and our formulas for the things themselves, manipulating facts so that we see only what conveniently fits our prejudices. Zen uses language against itself to blast out these preconceptions and to destroy the specious "reality" in our minds so that we can *see directly.* Zen is saying, as Wittgenstein said, "Don't think: Look!"

Since the Zen intuition seeks to awaken a direct metaphysical consciousness beyond the empirical, reflecting, knowing, willing and talking ego, this awareness must be immediately present to itself and not mediated by either conceptual or reflexive or imaginative knowledge. And yet far from being mere negation, Zen is also entirely positive. Let us hear D.T. Suzuki on the subject:

> "Zen always aims at grasping the central fact of life, which can never be brought to the dissecting table of the intellect. To grasp the central fact of life, Zen is forced to propose a series of negations. Mere negation however is not the spirit of Zen . . ." (Hence, he says, the Zen Masters neither affirm nor negate, they simply act or speak in such a way that the action or speech itself is a plain fact bursting with Zen. . . .) Suzuki continues: "When the spirit of Zen is grasped in its purity, it will be seen what a real thing that (act—in this case a slap) is. For here is no negation, no affirmation, but a plain fact, a pure experience, the very foundation of our being and thought. All the quietness and emptiness one might desire in the midst of most active meditation lies therein. Do not be carried away by anything outward or conventional. Zen must be seized with bare hands, with no gloves on." (D.T. Suzuki, *Introduction to Zen Buddhism,* London. 1960, p. 51)

It is in this sense that "Zen teaches nothing; it merely enables us to wake up and become aware. It does not teach, it points." (Suzuki *Introduction,* p. 38) The acts and gestures of a Zen Master are no more "statements" than is the ringing of an alarm clock.

All the words and actions of the Zen Masters and of their disciples are to be understood in this context. Usually the Master is simply "producing facts" which the disciple either sees or does not see.

Many of the Zen stories, which are almost always incomprehensible in rational terms, are simply the ringing of an alarm clock, and the reaction of the sleeper. Usually the misguided sleeper makes a response which in effect turns off the alarm so that he can go back to sleep. Sometimes he jumps out of bed with a shout of astonishment that it is so late. Sometimes he just sleeps and does not hear the alarm at all!

In so far as the disciple takes the fact to be a sign of something else, he is misled by it. The Master may (by means of some other fact) try to make him aware of this. Often it is precisely at the point where the disciple realizes himself to be utterly misled that he also realizes everything else along with it: chiefly, of course, that there was nothing to realize in the first place except the fact. What *fact?* If you know the answer you are awake. You hear the alarm!

But we in the West, living in a tradition of stubborn egocentered practicality and geared entirely for the use and manipulation of everything, always pass from one thing to another, from cause to effect, from the first to the next and to the last and then back to the first. Everything always points to something else, and hence we never stop anywhere because we cannot: as soon as we pause, the escalator reaches the end of the ride and we have to get off and find another one. Nothing is allowed just to be and to mean itself: everything has to mysteriously signify something else. Zen is especially designed to frustrate the mind that thinks in such terms. The

Zen "fact," whatever it may be, always lands across our road like a fallen tree beyond which we cannot pass.

Nor are such facts lacking in Christianity—the Cross for example. Just as the Buddha's "Fire Sermon" radically transforms the Buddhist's awareness of all that is around him, so the "word of the Cross" in very much the same way gives the Christian a radically new consciousness of the meaning of his life and of his relationship with other men and with the world around him.

In both cases, the "facts" are not merely impersonal and objective, but facts of personal experience. Both Buddhism and Christianity are alike in making use of ordinary everyday human existence as material for a radical transformation of consciousness. Since ordinary everyday human existence is full of confusion and suffering, then obviously one will make good use of both of these in order to transform one's awareness and one's understanding, and to go beyond both to attain "wisdom" in love. It would be a grave error to suppose that Buddhism and Christianity merely offer various *explanations* of suffering, or worse, justifications and mystifications built on this ineluctable fact. On the contrary both show that suffering remains inexplicable most of all for the man who attempts *to explain it in order to evade it,* or who thinks explanation itself is an escape. Suffering is not a "problem" as if it were something we could stand outside and control. Suffering, as both Christianity and Buddhism see, each in its own way, is part of our very ego-identity and empirical existence, and the only thing to do about it is to plunge right into the middle of contradiction and confusion in order to be transformed by what Zen calls the "Great Death" and Christianity calls "dying and rising with Christ."

Let us now return to the obscure and tantalizing "facts" in which Zen deals. In the relation between Zen Master and disciple, the most usually encountered "fact" is the disciple's frustration, his inability to get somewhere by the use of his own will and his own reasoning. Most sayings of the Zen Masters deal with this situation, and try to convey to the disciple that he has a fundamentally misleading experience of himself and of his capacities.

"When the cart stops," said Huai-Jang, the Master of Ma-Tsu, "do you whip the cart or whip the ox?" And he added, "If one sees the Tao from the standpoint of making and unmaking, or gathering and scattering, one does not really see the Tao."

If this remark about whipping the cart or the ox is obscure, perhaps another *Mondo* (question and answer) will suggest the same fact in a different way.

> A monk asks Pai-Chang, "Who is the Buddha?"
> Pai-Chang answers: "Who are you?"

A monk wants to know what is *Prajna* (the metaphysical wisdom-intuition of Zen). Not only that, but *Mahaprajna,* Great or Absolute Wisdom. The whole works.
The Master answers without concern:
> "The snow is falling fast and all is enveloped in mist."
> The monk remains silent.
> The Master asks: "Do you understand?"
> "No, Master, I do not."
> Thereupon the Master composed a verse for him:

> *Mahaprajna*
> It is neither taking in nor giving up.
> If one understands it not,
> The wind is cold, the snow is falling.
> (Suzuki, *Introduction,* p. 99-100)

The monk is "trying to understand" when in fact he ought to try to *look*. The apparently mysterious and cryptic sayings of Zen become much simpler when we see them in the whole context of Buddhist "mindfulness" or awareness, which in its most elementary form consists in that "bare attention" which simply *sees* what is right there and does not add any comment, any interpretation, any judgment, any conclusion. It just *sees*. Learning to see in this manner is the basic and fundamental exercise of Buddhist meditation. (See Nyanaponika Thero-Colombo, *The Heart of Buddhist Meditation*, Celon, 1956)

If one reaches the point where understanding fails, this is not a tragedy: it is simply a reminder to stop thinking and start looking. Perhaps there is nothing to figure out after all: perhaps we only need to wake up.

A monk said: "I have been with you (Master), for a long time, and yet I am unable to understand your way. How is this?"

The Master said: "Where you do not understand, there is the point for your understanding."

"How is understanding possible when it is impossible?"

The Master said: "The cow gives birth to a baby elephant; clouds of dust rise over the ocean." (Suzuki, *Introduction*, p. 116)

In more technical language, and therefore perhaps more comprehensibly for us, Suzuki says: "Prajna is pure act, pure experience . . . it has a distinct noetic quality . . . but it is not rationalistic . . . it is characterized by immediacy . . . it must not be identified with ordinary intuition . . . for in the case of prajna intuition there is no definable object to be intuited. . . . In prajna intuition the object of intuition is never a concept postulated by an elaborate process of reasoning; it is never 'this' or 'that'; it does not want to attach itself to one particular object." (D.T. Suzuki, *Studies in Zen*, London 1957, p. 87-9) For this reason, Suzuki concludes that *Prajna* intuition is different from "the kind of intuition we have generally in reli-

53

gious and philosophical discourses" in which God or the Absolute are objects of intuition and "the act of intuition is considered complete when a state of identification takes place between the object and the subject." (Suzuki, *Studies* p. 89)

This is not the place to discuss the very interesting and complex question raised here. Let us only say that it is by no means certain that the religious, or at any rate mystical, intuition always sees God "as object." And in fact we shall see that Suzuki qualifies this opinion quite radically by admitting that the mystical intuition of Eckhart is the same as *Prajna*.

Leaving this question aside, it must be said here that if anyone tries to spell out a philosophical or doctrinal interpretation for the Zen sayings like those we have quoted above, he is mistaken. If he seeks to argue that when Pai Chang points to the falling snow as answer to a question about the Absolute, as though to say that the falling snow were identified with the Absolute, in other words that this intuition was a reflexive pantheistic awareness of the *Absolute as object,* seen in the falling snow, then he has entirely missed the point of Zen. To imagine that Zen is "teaching pantheism" is to imagine that it is trying to explain something. We repeat: Zen explains nothing. It just sees. Sees what? Not an Absolute Object but Absolute Seeing.

Though this may seem very remote from Christianity, which is definitely a message, we must nevertheless remember the importance of *direct experience* in the Bible. All forms of "knowing," especially in the religious sphere, and especially where God is concerned, are valid in proportion as they are a matter of experience and of intimate contact. We are all familiar with the Biblical expression "to know" in the sense of to possess in the act of love. This is not the place to examine the possible Zenlike analogies in the experiences of the Old Testament prophets. They were certainly as factual, as existential and as disconcerting as any fact of Zen! Nor can we more than indicate briefly here the well-known importance of direct experience in the New Testament. This is of course to be sought above all in the revelation of the Holy Spirit, the mysterious Gift in which God becomes one with the Believer in order to know and love Himself in the Believer.

In the first two chapters of the first Epistle to the Corinthians St. Paul distinguishes between two kinds of wisdom: one which consists in the knowledge of words and statements, a rational, dialectical wisdom, and another which is at once a matter of paradox and of experience, and goes beyond the reach of reason. To attain to this spiritual wisdom, one must first be liberated from servile dependence on the "wisdom of speech." (I Cor. 1:17) This liberation is effected by the "word of the Cross" which makes no sense to those who cling to their own familiar views and habits of thought and is a means by which God "destroys the wisdom of the wise." (I Cor. 1: 18-23) The word of the Cross is in fact completely baffling and disconcerting both to the Greeks with their philosophy and to the Jews with their well-interpreted Law. But when one has been freed from dependence on verbal formulas and conceptual structures, the Cross becomes a source of "power." This power emanates from the "foolishness of God" and it also makes use of "foolish instruments." (the Apostles). (I Cor. 1: 27 ff.) On the other hand, he who can accept this paradoxical "foolishness" experiences in himself a secret and mysterious power, which is the power of Christ living in him as the ground of a totally new life and a new being. (I Cor. 2:1-4, cf. Eph. 1:18-23, Gal. 6:14-16)

Here it is essential to remember that for a Christian "the word of the Cross" is nothing theoretical, but a stark and existential experience of union with Christ in His death in order to share in His resurrection. To fully "hear" and "receive" the word of the Cross means much more than simple assent to the dogmatic proposition that Christ died for our sins. It means to be "nailed to the Cross with Christ," so that the ego-self is no longer the principle of our deepest actions, which now proceed from Christ living in us. "I live, now not I, but Christ lives in me." (Gal. 2:19-20; see also Romans 8:5-17) To receive the word of the Cross means the acceptance of a complete self-emptying, a *Kenosis,* in union with the self-emptying of Christ "obedient unto death." (Phil. 2:5-11) It is essential to true Christianity that this experience of the Cross and of self-emptying be central in the life of the Christian so that he may fully receive the Holy Spirit and know (again by experience) all the riches of God in and through Christ. (John 14:16-17, 26; 15:26-27; 16:7-15)

When Gabriel Marcel says: "There are thresholds which thought alone, left to itself, can never permit us to cross. An experience is required—an experience of poverty and sickness . . . ." (Quoted, A. Gelin, *Les Pauvres de Yahvé,* Paris, 1954, p. 57) he is stating a simple Christian truth in terms familiar to Zen.

We must never forget that Christianity is much more than the intellectual acceptance of a religious message by a blind and submissive faith which never understands what the message means except in terms of authoritative interpretations handed down externally by experts in the name of the Church. On the contrary, faith is the door to the full inner life of the Church, a life which includes not only access to an authoritative teaching but above all to a deep personal experience which is at once unique and yet shared by the whole Body of Christ, in the Spirit of Christ. St. Paul compares this knowledge of God, in the Spirit, to the subjective knowledge that a man has of himself. Just as no one can know my inner self except my own "spirit," so no one can know God except God's Spirit; yet this Holy Spirit is given to us, in such a way that God knows Himself in us, and this experience is utterly real, though it cannot be communicated in terms understandable to those who do not share it. (See I Cor. 2:7-15.) Consequently, St. Paul concludes, "we have the mind of Christ." (I Cor. 2:16)

Now when we see that for Buddhism *Prajna* is describable as "having the Buddha mind" we understand that there must surely be some possibility of finding an analogy somewhere between Buddhist and Christian experience, though we are now speaking more in terms of doctrine than of pure experience. Yet the doctrine is about the experience. We cannot push our investigation further here, but it is significant that Suzuki, reading the following lines from Eckhart (which are perfectly orthodox and traditional Catholic theology), said they were *"the same as Prajna intuition."* (D.T. Suzuki, *Mysticism: East and West,* p. 40; the quotation from C. de B. Evans' translation of Eckhart, London, 1924, p. 147)

"In giving us His love God has given us the Holy Ghost so that we can love Him with the love wherewith He loves Himself." The Son Who, in us, loves the Father, in the Spirit, is translated thus by Suzuki into Zen terms: "one mirror reflecting another with no shadow between them." (Suzuki, *Mysticism: East and West,* p. 41)

Suzuki also frequently quotes a sentence of Eckhart's: "The eye wherein I see God is the same eye wherein God sees me" (Suzuki, *Mysticism: East and West,* p. 50) as an exact expression of what Zen means by *Prajna.*

Whether or not Dr. Suzuki's interpretation of the text in Zen terms is theologically perfect in every way remains to be seen, though at first sight there seems to be no reason why it should not be thoroughly acceptable. What is important for us here is that the interpretation is highly suggestive and interesting in itself, reflecting a kind of intuitive affinity for Christian mysticism. Furthermore it is highly significant that a Japanese thinker schooled in Zen should be so open to what is basically the most obscure and difficult mystery of Christian theology: the dogma of the Trinity and the mission of the Divine Persons in the Christian and in the Church. This would seem to indicate that the real area for investigation of analogies and correspondences between Christianity and Zen might after all be theology rather than psychology or asceticism. At least theology is not excluded, but it must be theology as experienced in Christian contemplation, not the speculative theology of textbooks and disputations.

The few words that have been written in this introduction, and the brief, bare suggestions it contains, are by no means intended as an adequate "comparison" between Christian experience and Zen experience. Obviously, we have done little more than express a pious hope that a common ground can some day be found. But at least this should make the Western and Christian reader more ready to enter this book with an open mind, and perhaps help him to suspend judgment for a while, and not decide immediately that Zen is so esoteric and so outlandish that it has no interest or importance for us. On the contrary, Zen has much to teach the West, and recently Dom Aelred Graham, in a book which became deservedly popular (Graham, *Zen Catholicism,* N.Y., 1963), pointed out that there was not a little in Zen that was pertinent to our own ascetic and religious practice. It is quite possible for Zen to be adapted and used to clear the air of ascetic irrelevancies and help us to regain a healthy natural balance in our understanding of the spiritual life.

But Zen must be grasped in its simple reality, not rationalized or imagined in terms of some fantastic and esoteric interpretation of human existence.

Though few Westerners will ever actually come to a real understanding of Zen, it is still worth their while to be exposed to its brisk and heady atmosphere.

# D.T. SUZUKI: THE MAN AND HIS WORK

*"On peut se sentir fier d'être contemporain
d'un certain nombre d'hommes de ce temps. . . ."*
ALBERT CAMUS.

We live in an unusual age. It is therefore no great wonder
that there have been unusual men in it. Though perhaps
less universally known than such figures as Einstein and
Gandhi (who became symbols of our time) Daisetz Suzuki
was no less remarkable a man than these. And though his
work may not have had such resounding and public effect, he
contributed no little to the spiritual and intellectual revolution
of our time. The impact of Zen on the West, striking with its
fullest force right after World War II, in the midst of the
existentialist upheaval, at the beginning of the atomic and
cybernetic age, with Western religion and philosophy in a
state of crisis and with the consciousness of man threatened
by the deepest alienation, the work and personal influence of
Dr. Suzuki proved to be both timely and fruitful—much
more fruitful than we have perhaps begun to realize. I do
not speak now of the rather superficial Western enthusiasm
for the externals and the froth of Zen (which Dr. Suzuki
himself could tolerantly but objectively evaluate) but of the
active leaven of Zen insight which he brought into the already
bubbling ferment of Western thinking in his contacts with
psychoanalysis, philosophy, and religious thought like that of
Paul Tillich.

First published in *The Eastern Buddhist* (New Series) Volume II, No.
1, (Otani University, Kyoto, Japan) August, 1967.

There is no question that Dr. Suzuki brought to this age of dialogue a very special gift of his own: a capacity to apprehend and to occupy the precise standpoints where communication could hope to be most effective. He was able to do this all the more effectively because one felt he was entirely free from the dictates of partisan thought-patterns and academic ritualism. He was not compelled to play the complex games by which one jockeys for advantage in the intellectual world. Therefore, of course, he found himself quite naturally and without difficulty in a position of prominence. He spoke with authority, the authority of a simple, clear-sighted man who was aware of human limits and not inclined to improve on them with huge artificial structures that had no real significance. He did not need to put another head on top of his own, as the Zen saying goes. This of course is an advantage in any dialogue, for when men try to communicate with each other, it is good for them to speak with distinct and personal voices, not to blur their identities by speaking through several official masks at the same time.

It was my good fortune to meet Dr. Suzuki and to have a couple of all too short conversations with him. The experience was not only rewarding, but I would say it was unforgettable. It was, in my own life, a quite extraordinary event since, because of the circumstances in which I live, I do not get to meet all those I would meet professionally if I were, say, teaching in a university. I had known his work for a long time, had corresponded with him, and we had had a short dialogue published, in which we discussed the "Wisdom of Emptiness" as found comparatively in Zen and in the Egyptian Desert Fathers. (see p. 99) On his last trip to the United States I had the great privilege and pleasure of meeting him. One had to meet this man in order fully to appreciate him. He seemed to me to embody all the indefinable qualities of the

"Superior Man" of the ancient Asian, Taoist, Confucian and Buddhist traditions. Or rather in meeting him one seemed to meet that "True Man of No Title" that Chuang Tzu and the Zen Masters speak of. And of course this is the man one really wants to meet. Who else is there? In meeting Dr. Suzuki and drinking a cup of tea with him I felt I had met this one man. It was like finally arriving at one's own home. A very happy experience, to say the least. There is not a great deal one has to say about it, because to speak at length would divert attention to details that are after all irrelevant. When one is actually there with a person, the multiple details fall naturally into the unity that is seen without being expressed. When one speaks of it secondhand there are only the multiple details. The True Man has meanwhile long since gone about his business somewhere else.

Thus far I have spoken simply as a human being. I should also speak as a Catholic, as a man formed by a certain Western religious tradition but with, I hope, a legitimate curiosity about and openness to other traditions. Such a one can only with diffidence hazard statements about Buddhism, since he cannot be sure that he has a trustworthy insight into the spiritual values of a tradition with which he is not really familiar. Speaking for myself, I can venture to say that in Dr. Suzuki, Buddhism finally became for me completely comprehensible, whereas before it had been a very mysterious and confusing jumble of words, images, doctrines, legends, rituals, buildings, and so forth. It seemed to me that the great and baffling cultural luxuriance which has clothed the various forms of Buddhism in different parts of Asia is the beautiful garment thrown over something quite simple. The greatest religions are all, in fact, very simple. They all retain very important essential differences, no doubt, but in their inner reality Christianity, Buddhism, Islam and Judaism are extremely simple (though capable, as I say, of baffling luxuriance) and they all end up with the simplest and most baffling thing of all: direct confrontation with Absolute Being, Absolute Love, Absolute Mercy or Absolute Void, by an immediate and fully awakened engagement in the living of everyday life. In Christianity the confrontation is theological and affective, through word and love. In Zen it is metaphysical and intellectual, through insight and emptiness. Yet Christianity too has its tradition of apophatic contemplation of knowledge in "unknowing," while the last words I remember Dr. Suzuki saying (before the usual good-byes) were "The most important thing is Love!" I must say that as a Christian I was profoundly moved. Truly *Prajna* and *Karuna* are one (as the Buddhist says), or *Caritas* (love) is indeed the highest knowledge.

I saw Dr. Suzuki only in two brief visits and I did not feel I ought to waste time exploring abstract, doctrinal explanations of his tradition. But I did feel that I was speaking to someone who, in a tradition completely different from my own, had matured, had become complete and found his way. One cannot understand Buddhism until one meets it in this existential manner, in a person in whom it is alive. Then there is no longer a problem of understanding doctrines which cannot help being a bit exotic for a Westerner, but only a question of appreciating a value which is self-evident. I am sure that no alert and intelligent Westerner ever met Dr. Suzuki without something of the same experience.

This same existential quality is evident in another way in Dr. Suzuki's vast published work. An energetic, original and productive worker, granted the gift of a long life and tireless enthusiasm for his subject, he has left us a whole library of Zen in English. I am unfortunately not familiar with his work in Japanese or able to say what it amounts to. But what we have in English is certainly without question the most complete and most authentic presentation of an Asian tradition and experience by any one man in terms accessible to the West. The uniqueness of Dr. Suzuki's work lies in the directness with which an Asian thinker has been able to communicate his own experience of a profound and ancient tradition in a Western language. This is quite a different proposition from the more or less trustworthy translations of Eastern texts by Western scholars with no experience of Asian spiritual values, or even the experience of Asian traditions acquired by Westerners.

One reason for the peculiar effectiveness of Dr. Suzuki's communication of Zen to the West is that he had a rather remarkable capacity to transpose Zen into the authentic terms of Western mystical traditions that were most akin to it. I do not know how deep an acquaintance Dr. Suzuki had with the Western mystics, but he had read Meister Eckhart pretty thoroughly. (I may mention in parentheses that I agree with Dr. Suzuki in his final position about Zen and mysticism, in which he elected to say that Zen was "not mysticism" in order to avoid certain disastrous ambiguities. But this question still calls for further study.)

Although Dr. Suzuki accepted the current rather superficial Western idea of Eckhart as a unique and completely heretical phenomenon, we must admit, with more recent scholarship, that Eckhart does represent a profound, wide and largely orthodox current in Western religious thought: that which goes back to Plotinus and Pseudo-Dionysius and comes down in the West through Scotus Erigena and the medieval school of St. Victor, but also profoundly affected Eckhart's master, St. Thomas Aquinas. Having come in touch with this relatively little-known tradition Suzuki found it congenial and was able to make good use of it. I found for example that in my dialogue with him (see page 99), he was able to use the mythical language in which the Fall of Man is described, in the Bible and the Church Fathers, to distinct advantage psychologically and spiritually. He spoke quite naturally and easily of the implications of the "Fall" in terms of man's alienation from himself, and he did so in just the same simple natural way as the Fathers of the Church like St. Augustine or St. Gregory of Nyssa did. If the truth be told, there is a great deal in common in the psychological and spiritual insight of the Church Fathers and in the psychoanalytically oriented Christian existential thinking of men like Tillich, himself more influenced than many realized by the Augustinian tradition. Dr. Suzuki was perfectly at home in this atmosphere and perfectly able to handle these traditional symbols. In fact he was far more at home with them than many Western theologians. He understood and appreciated the symbolic language of the Bible and the Fathers much more directly than many of our contemporaries, Catholics included, for whom all this is little more than an embarrassment. The whole reality of the "Fall" is inscribed in our nature in what Jung called symbolic archetypes, and the Fathers of the Church (as well as the Biblical writers too no doubt) were much more concerned with this archetypal significance than with the Fall as an "historical event." Others besides Dr. Suzuki have, without being Christians, intuitively grasped the importance of this symbol. Two names spring to mind: Erich Fromm, the psychoanalyst, and that remarkable and too-little known poet Edwin Muir, the translator into English of Franz Kafka. I do not think Dr. Suzuki was the kind of person to be bothered with any concern about whether or not he was sufficiently "modern." The True Man of No Title is not concerned about such labels, since he knows no time but the present, and knows he cannot apprehend either the past or the future except in the present.

It may be said that all Dr. Suzuki's books are pretty much about the same thing. Occasionally he will draw back and view Zen from the standpoint of culture, or psychoanalysis, or from the viewpoint of Christian mysticism (in Eckhart), but even then he does not really move out of Zen into some other field, or even take a radically new look at his subject. He says very much the same things, tells the same wonderful Zen stories perhaps in slightly different words, and ends with the same conclusion: zero equals infinity. Yet there is no monotony in his works and one does not feel he is repeating himself, because in fact each book is brand new. Each book is a whole new experience. Those of us who have written a great deal can well admire this quality in Dr. Suzuki's work: its remarkable consistency, its unity.

Pseudo-Dionysius says that the wisdom of the contemplative moves in a *motus orbicularis*—a circling and hovering motion like that of the eagle above some invisible quarry, or the turning of a planet around an invisible sun. The work of Dr. Suzuki bears witness of the silent orbiting of *Prajna* which is (in the language of the same Western tradition of the Pseudo-Areopagite and Erigena), a "circle whose circumference is nowhere and whose center is everywhere." The rest of us travel in linear flight. We go far, take up distant positions, abandon them, fight battles and then wonder what we got so excited about, construct systems and then junk them, and wander all over continents looking for something new. Dr. Suzuki stayed right where he was, in his own Zen, and found it inexhaustibly new with each new book. Surely this is an indication of a special gift, a special quality of spiritual genius.

In any event, his work remains with us as a great gift, as one of the unique spiritual and intellectual achievements of our time. It is above all precious to us in the way it has moved

East and West closer together, bringing Japan and America into agreement on a deep level, when everything seems to conspire to breed conflict, division, incomprehension, confusion and war. Our time has not always excelled in the works of peace. We can be proud of a contemporary who has devoted his life to those works, and does so with such success.

# NISHIDA: A ZEN PHILOSOPHER

The eminent Japanese philosopher Kitaro Nishida (1870-1945) did for Zen Buddhism a work analogous to that of Jacques Maritain in Catholic philosophy; he constructed, within his own mystical tradition, and on the basis of its traditional and spiritual intuitions, a philosophy which at the same time speaks to modern—even Western—man, and remains open to the highest wisdom which it seeks in union with God. Dr. Daisetz Suzuki has rightly said that it is difficult to understand Nishida unless one has some acquaintance with Zen. On the other hand, some knowledge of existentialist phenomenology may serve as a preparation for understanding the only book of Nishida thus far translated into English—his first work: *A Study of Good* (translated by V. H. Viglielmo, Printing Bureau, Japanese Government, Japanese National Commission for UNESCO, 1960)

Like Merleau-Ponty, Nishida is concerned with the primary structure of consciousness, and seeks to preserve the unity that exists between the consciousness and the outer world reflected in it. The starting point of Nishida is a "pure experience" a "direct experience" of undifferentiated unity which is quite the opposite to the starting point of Descartes in his *cogito*.

Descartes finds his basic intuition in the reflexive self-awareness of the individual thinking subject, standing, as it were, outside of and apart from other objects of knowledge. From the starting point of reflexive thought the subject takes the abstract concepts of itself and of its own being as objects —*cogito ergo sum*. For Nishida (as, in another context, for

Maritain) what comes first is the *unifying* intuition of the *basic unity of subject and object in being* or a deep "grasp of life" in its existential concreteness "at the base of consciousness." This basic unity is not an abstract concept but being itself—charged with the dynamism of spirit and of love. In this sense one might venture to say that Nishida's starting point is *sum ergo cogito*. But one must always take this with a tantalizing grain of Zen salt. "I am," but *who* is this "I?" The fundamental reality is neither external nor internal, objective nor subjective. It is prior to all differentiations and contradictions. Zen calls it emptiness, *Sunyata*, or "suchness." The mature grasp of the primordial emptiness in which all things are one is *Prajna*, wisdom.

This wisdom is the direct experience not of the "One" and the "Absolute" in the abstract, but of "the Self" or "the Buddha nature." For this unitive awareness which Nishida sees as a union *of love*, he uses the term "Spirit."

Nishida is too good a Zen-man to simply reduce everything to an abstract original unity and leave it to dissolve there. This, as he repeatedly says, would be a betrayal of reality and of life. Out of the original undifferentiated oneness of pure experience, contradictions must develop, and through conflict and contradiction the mind and will of man must work their way strenuously to a higher unity in which the primitive "direct experience" is now manifested on a higher level. Here contradictions and conflicts are resolved in a transcendent unity which is, in fact, a religious experience. Nishida uses the term "mystical" to describe it. Other Zen writers have avoided this particular term, which they consider misleading.

Perhaps the most original, indeed the most revolutionary, aspect of Nishida's thought, at least from the Buddhist viewpoint, is his *personalism*.

The conclusion of his *A Study of Good* is that, in fact, the highest good is the *good of the person*. This may seem at first sight to be a direct contradiction of the basic tenets of the Buddhist Religion. Buddha taught that all evil is rooted in the "ignorance" which makes us take our individual ego as our true self. But Nishida is not confusing the "person" with the external and individual self. Nor is the "person" for him simply the "subject" related to various objects, or even to God in an I–Thou relationship. The root of personality is to be sought in the "true Self" which is manifested in the basic unification of consciousness in which subject and object are one. Hence the highest good is "the self's fusion with the highest reality." Human personality is regarded as the force which effects this fusion. The hopes and desires of the external, individual self are all, in fact, opposed to this higher unity. They are centered on the affirmation of the individual. It is only at the point where the hopes and fears of the individual self are done away with and forgotten "that the true human personality appears." In a word, realization of the human personality in this highest spiritual sense is for us the good toward which all life is to be oriented. It is even the "absolute good," in so far as the human personality is, for Nishida, intimately and probably even essentially related to the personality of God.

This is another quite revolutionary thesis in Buddhism. Nishida definitely and clearly states that the "deepest demand of man's heart" or the "religious demand" is the quest for a *personal* God. This demand does not lead to the ultimate satisfaction of individual aspirations: on the contrary, it requires their sacrifice and death. The individual self must cease to assert himself as a "center of unification" and of consciousness. God Himself, the personal God, is the *deepest center* of consciousness and unification (remember the use of this expression by St. John of the Cross). To fully realize this, not by quietistic annihilation and immersion but by the active and creative awareness of love, is our highest good.

For the Christian philosopher, a problem is posed by the fact that while God, in Nishida, is explicitly personal, he is also explicitly pantheistic, and becomes the Spirit of unity and truth at the center of the universe, a kind of *anima mundi*. But to one who is familiar with Eastern thought, it will be seen that what constitutes for us a philosophical confusion arises from the breakthrough of purely religious and mystical thought into the philosophical structure, which then becomes an extrapolation of profound spiritual experience.

The Christian thinker will certainly not lose sight of perspectives and distinctions which have been developed in his own tradition but have never been felt necessary in the East. The advent of technical philosophical thought in the Western sense is something quite new in Japan. Traditionally, Eastern philosophies tend to combine philosophical, religious thought with concrete expressions of spiritual experience. What is important is that, in terms of a pantheist metaphysic, Nishida Kitaro is expressing religious intuitions of great purity and profundity which resemble those of some of the great contemplative thinkers of our own tradition. The closing lines of the book may serve to remind us of this fact.

"God is not someone who must be known according to analysis and reasoning. If we consider that the essence of reality is a personal thing, God is that which is most personal. Our knowing God is only possible through the intuition of love or faith. Therefore we who say we do not know God but only love Him and believe in Him are the ones who are most able to know God."

We would miss the point of Nishida's thought entirely if we did not grasp its profoundly religious and "mystical" spirit. His conclusions as to the highest good are summed up already in a sentence from an early diary: "If my heart can become pure and simple like that of a child, I think there probably can be no greater happiness than this."

# TRANSCENDENT EXPERIENCE

WHO IS IT THAT HAS A TRANSCENDENT EXPERIENCE?

The purpose of this note is to raise an important question, in fact to cast a serious doubt upon assumptions which, casually taken for granted, make all discussion of the transcendent experience, especially "mystical" experience, completely ambiguous. This ambiguity is bound to sterilize and frustrate the disciplines or other means used to "attain" the transcendent experience.

First of all, what is meant by *transcendent experience?* The term is unsatisfactory, but it intends to narrow the field: transcendent experience is something more definite than "peak experience." It is an experience of metaphysical or mystical self-transcending and also at the same time an experience of the "Transcendent" or the "Absolute" or "God" not so much as object but Subject. The Absolute Ground of Being (and beyond that the Godhead as "Urgrund" i.e. as infinite uncircumscribed freedom) is realized so to speak "from within"— realized from within "Himself" and from within "myself," though "myself" is now lost and "found" "in Him." These metaphorical expressions all point to the problem we have in mind: the problem of a self that is "no-self," that is by no means an "alienated self" but on the contrary a transcendent Self which, to clarify it in Christian terms, is metaphysically distinct from the Self of God and yet perfectly identified with

This essay first published and copyrighted by the R.M. Bucke Memorial Society's (Montreal) *Newsletter-Review* Volume I, No. 2, September, 1966.

that Self by love and freedom, so that there appears to be but one Self. Experience of this is what we here call "transcendent experience" or the illumination of wisdom (*Sapientia, Sophia, Prajna*). To attain this experience is to penetrate the reality of all that is, to grasp the meaning of one's own existence, to find one's true place in the scheme of things, to relate perfectly to all that is in a relation of identity and love.

What this *is not:*

It is not a regressive immersion in nature, the cosmos or "pure being," in narcissistic tranquillity, a happy loss of identity in a warm, regressive, dark, oceanic swoon. It is not precisely identifiable with erotic peak experiences even where these are authentically personal rather than (in Fromm's sense) symbiotic. It is more than aesthetic transcendence, though it can combine with it and lift it to a higher point of metaphysical insight (as in Zen painting). It is also more than moral transcendence, the experience of that heroic generosity in self-giving which takes us beyond and above our own limits: but of course it can combine with or emerge from moral heroism, lifting it to the plane of a mystical self-sacrifice and self-giving.

It is finally beyond the ordinary level of religious or spiritual experience (authentic experience of course) in which the intelligence and "the heart" (a traditional and technical term in Sufism, Hesychasm and Christian mysticism generally) are illumined with insight into the meaning of revelation, or of being, or of life. All these experiences are on a level where the self-aware subject remains more or less conscious of himself as subject, and indeed his awareness of his subjectivity is heightened and purified.

But in the transcendent experience there is a radical and revolutionary change in the subject. This change must not be confused with psychological regression, though at times the impact on the psyche and organism may be such that "blinded by excessive light" it is afflicted and beaten back into a kind of regressive darkness, in preparation for the leap into pure transcendence, freedom, light, love and grace.

*Who is it that has this experience?*

Very often, descriptions and discussions of this experience seem to take for granted that the only subject of it is the ego-self, the individual person. We assume that this empirical ego, who is able to be aware of itself and affirm itself as "I am" (indeed "I have experiences therefore I am"), is at once the subject and beneficiary of transcendent experiences. These become the crowning glory of egohood and self-fulfillment. We doubtless admit that in transcending itself the ego does indeed go "beyond" itself, but in the end this proof of spiritual elasticity is all to its own credit. The further it can go without snapping, the better and more respectable an ego it is. In fact, the ego trains itself to be so completely elastic that it can stretch itself almost to the vanishing point and still come back and chalk up another experience on the score card. In this case, however, there is no real self-transcendence. The "trip" that is taken is ultimately a release for and an intensification of ego-consciousness.

The following remarks need perhaps to be made about this way of describing the transcendent experience:

1) It may be satisfactory if all one wants to describe is an experience on the aesthetic or even moral level. But as soon as this kind of language is used to express a transcendent religious or metaphysical experience, such as mystical ecstasy, Zen *Satori,* and so on, it not only becomes misleading but it involves our thought in irreconcilable contradictions.

2) For this very reason it is basic to Zen, to Sufism and to Christian mysticism (to mention only those approaches to transcendent experience with which the writer is familiar) *to radically and unconditionally question the ego which appears*

*to be the subject of the transcendent experience,* and thus of course to radically question the whole nature of the experience itself precisely as "experience." Are we any longer able to speak of an experience when the subject of the experience is not a limited, well-defined, empirical subject? Or, to put it in other words, are we able to speak of "consciousness" when the conscious subject is no longer able to be aware of itself as separate and unique? Then if the empirical ego is conscious at all, is it conscious of itself as transcended, left behind, irrelevant, illusory, and indeed as the root of all ignorance (*Avidya*)?

3) Once this has been stated we see that it throws light on the terms in which one can speak of such a transcendent experience as regressive. Even if one speaks of "regression in the service of the ego" it seems to have little or nothing to do with the authentically transcendent experience, which is a matter of *superconsciousness* rather than a lapse into preconsciousness or unconsciousness. (The Zen "unconscious" is metaphysical rather than psychological.) The traditional term in Christian mysticism, *raptus,* or "rapture," implies not the mode of being "carried away" that belongs properly to aesthetic or to erotic experience (though erotic imagery is used to describe it in certain types of Christian mysticism) but of being ontologically carried "above oneself" (*supra se*). In the Christian tradition the focus of this "experience" is found not in the individual self as a separate, limited and temporal ego, but in Christ, or the Holy Spirit "within" this self. In Zen it is Self with a capital S, that is to say precisely *not* the ego-self. This Self is the Void.

It is true that statements about complete annihilation of the ego have always to be taken with serious qualifications and are apparently intended to be so taken, especially by Christian mystics, and yet it is evident that the *identity* or the *person* which is the subject of this transcendent consciousness is not the ego as isolated and contingent, but the person as "found" and "actualized" in union with Christ. In other words, in Christian mystical tradition the identity of the mystic is never purely and simply the mere empirical ego—still less the neurotic and narcissistic self—but the "person" who is identified with Christ, one with Christ. "I live now not I but Christ lives in me" (Gal. 2:20).

In the Christian tradition, then, we find this personal transcendence referred to as "having the mind of Christ" or knowing and seeing "in the Spirit of Christ," Spirit here being strictly personal, not just a vague reference to a certain inner emotional climate. This Spirit, who "fathoms everything even the abyss of God" and "understands the thoughts of God" as man understands his own heart, is "given us" in Christ as a transcendent superconsciousness of God and of "the Father" (see I Cor. 2, Romans 8, etc.).

More specifically, all transcendent experience is for the Christian a participation in "the mind of Christ"—"Let this mind be in you which was also in Christ Jesus . . . *who emptied himself* . . . obedient unto death. . . . Therefore God raised him and conferred upon him a name above all names." (Phil. 2:5-10) This dynamic of emptying and of transcendence accurately defines the transformation of the Christian consciousness in Christ. It is a kenotic transformation, an emptying of all the contents of the ego-consciousness to become a void in which the light of God or the glory of God, the full radiation of the infinite reality of His Being and Love are manifested.

Eckhart says in perfectly orthodox and traditional Christian terms, "In giving us His love God has given us His Holy Ghost so that we can love Him with the love wherewith He loves Himself. We love God with His own love; awareness of it deifies us." D.T. Suzuki quotes this with approval, comparing it with the *Prajna* wisdom of Zen. (Suzuki, *Mysticism: East and West*, p. 40)

Note that in Buddhism also the highest development of consciousness is that by which the individual ego is completely emptied and becomes identified with the enlightened Buddha, or rather finds itself to be in reality the enlightened Buddha mind. Nirvana is not the consciousness of an ego that is aware of itself as having crossed over to "the other shore" (to be on "another shore" is the same as not having crossed over), but the Absolute Ground-Consciousness of the Void, in which there are no shores. Thus the Buddhist enters into the self-emptying and enlightenment of Buddha as the Christian enters into the self-emptying (crucifixion) and glorification (resurrection and ascension) of Christ. The chief difference between the two is that the former is existential and onto-logical, the latter is theological and personal. But "person" here must be distinguished from "the individual empirical ego."

4) This explains why in all these higher religious traditions the path to transcendent realization is a path of ascetic self-emptying and "self-naughting" and not at all a path of self-affirmation, of self-fulfillment, or of "perfect attainment." That is why it is felt necessary by these traditions to speak in strong negative terms about what happens to the ego-subject, which instead of being "realized" in its own limited selfhood is spoken of rather as simply vanishing out of the picture altogether. The reason for this is not that the person loses his metaphysical or even physical status, or regresses into non-identity, but rather that his *real* status is quite other than what appears empirically to us to be his status. Hence it becomes overwhelmingly important for us *to become detached from our everyday conception of ourselves as potential subjects for special and unique experiences, or as candidates for realiza-*

*tion, attainment and fulfillment.* In other words, this means that a spiritual guide worth his salt will conduct a ruthless campaign against all forms of delusion arising out of spiritual ambition and self-complacency which aim to establish the ego in spiritual glory. That is why a St. John of the Cross is so hostile to visions, ecstasies and all forms of "special experience." That is why the Zen Masters say: "If you meet the Buddha, kill him."

Here we must be very circumspect. The "Holy Object" must be destroyed in so far as it is an idol embodying the secret desires, aspirations and powers of the ego-self. On the other hand it is futile and even deadly to simply sweep aside all other idols in order to confirm as absolute and ultimate the idol of an ego-self supposedly endowed with supreme autonomy and able to follow its own omnipotent spiritual whims. This is not spiritual freedom but ultimate narcissism.

Therefore there is a definite place for disciplines based on an I—Thou relationship between disciple and master, between the believer and his God. It is precisely in familiarity with liturgical worship and moral discipline that the beginner finds his identity, gains a certain confidence from his spiritual practice, and learns to believe that the spiritual life has a goal that is definitely possible of attainment. But the progressive must also learn to relax his grasp on his conception of what that goal is and "who it is" that will attain it. To cling too tenaciously to the "self" and its own fulfillment would guarantee that there would be no fulfillment at all.

As to the study of this whole question of "ego-self" and "person"—a matter of crucial importance for the dialogue between Eastern and Western religion—it must be carried on in the realm of metaphysics, and the ego as working hypothesis in psychology must not be confused with the metaphysical person which alone is capable of transcendent union with the

Ground of Being. The person in fact is rooted in that absolute Ground and not in the phenomenal contingency of egohood. Hence if the person were to attempt to go "outside" this metaphysical ground in order to experience himself as being and acting, or observe himself as an object functioning among other objects, the unitive wisdom experience would become impossible, because now the person is split in two—hence the paradox that as soon as there is "someone there" to have a transcendent experience, "the experience" is falsified and indeed becomes impossible.

# NIRVANA

So important is metaphysical insight in Buddhism, that it replaces theology and would make of Buddhism a religious philosophy rather than "a religion"—except that one stops short of such a definition. The expression "religious philosophy" would hardly account for the depth of the Buddhist experience, for which neither "religious" nor "philosophical" would seem to be a fully satisfactory epithet. Though there has been much philosophical speculation among various schools of Buddhism, the basic insight of Buddhism goes beyond speculation and renounces it. Sakyamuni (Buddha) himself refused to answer speculative questions, and he would not permit abstract philosophical discussion. His doctrine was not a doctrine but a way of being in the world. His religion was not a set of beliefs and convictions or of rites and sacraments, but an opening to love. His philosophy was not a world view but a significant silence, in which the fracture implied by conceptual knowledge was allowed to heal and reality appeared again in its mysterious "suchness."

Nevertheless, the basic insights of Buddhism are philosophical and metaphysical: they seek to penetrate the ground of Being and of knowledge, not by reasoning from abstract principles and axioms but by the purification and expansion of the moral and religious consciousness until it reaches a state of superconscious or metaconscious realization in which

This essay first published as foreword to "Marcel and Buddha: A Metaphysics of Enlightenment," by Sally Donnelly, in *Journal of Religious Thought,* (Howard University), Volume XXIV, No. 1, 1967-68.

subject and object become one. This realization or enlightenment is called *Nirvana*.

Obviously the best way to open a serious dialogue between Christian and Buddhist thought will be to discuss something of the nature of Buddhist enlightenment and to see whether some analogy to it can be found in Christian thought. Three main approaches offer themselves as more or less obvious: First, on the plane of mysticism and mystical experience. This may at first sight appear the most fruitful, but it is complicated by theological problems on the Christian side and by an absence of theological content which would offer material for comparison on the Buddhist side. Second there is the ethical level: Buddhist compassion is compared with Christian charity. But since Christian charity is a theological virtue, the same problem arises again here—the discussion takes place on two levels which fail to meet. Finally there is the plane of metaphysics. Here it would seem that a meeting is possible. The essay of Sally Donnelly encourages this particular hope, and we can be grateful to her for showing some very interesting analogies between the basic doctrines of Buddhism and the Christian existentialism of Gabriel Marcel. (I am aware that Marcel repudiated this label at the time of *Humani Generis* when all existentialism was in bad repute as being irreligious.)

From the metaphysical standpoint, Sally Donnelly shows us various ways in which Buddhist and Christian philosophical insights can be seen to correspond. On the basis of this correspondence, we are able to look a little further and envisage other possibilities of correspondence in the religious understanding of human existence and the practical conduct of life.

The special value of Sally Donnelly's study lies in its emphasis on *presence* in the world, which is common to Buddhism and Christianity. The Buddhist ideas of *Dharma* (a word almost untranslatable, somewhat akin to logos) and of *Tatatha* ("suchness") imply a realization of presence, and *Nirvana* is a matter of "pure presence" rather than of absence and negation. The meaning of life is found in openness to being and "being present" in full awareness.

Buddhist enlightenment, or *Nirvana,* the highest goal of man, has been completely misunderstood in the West. Perhaps this is because the concept of *Nirvana* first reached the West in translations of ascetic texts of the Little Vehicle, which emphasized the extinction of desire and the negative aspect of Buddhist enlightenment. This was taken up by romantic pessimists like Schopenhauer, and as a result the Western stereotype of Buddhism is that of the world-denying religion par excellence, in which the ideal is to spend one's earthly existence in a trance in order that after death one may pass away into pure nothingness. According to this view, all positive value in earthly existence is merely negated. It is difficult to conceive how such a supposed cult of inertia and death could have inspired such manifest evidences of vitality and joy as we find in Buddhist art, literature and culture generally all over the Far East.

In reality this distortion is rather similar to the distortion suffered by Christian mystics like St. John of the Cross, who is regarded as a life-denying and world-hating ascetic when in reality his mysticism superabounds in love, vitality and joy. The truth is that a certain kind of mentality cannot bear to have the worldly and the temporal called into question in any way whatever—any attempt to say that these values remain relative and contingent is rejected as Manichean denigration of the lovely earth. But if earthly and temporal values are treated in fact as absolutes, who can enjoy them? They become distorted and unreal and the person who sees them through this delusion is incapable of grasping the real value which they contain. The tragedy of a life centered on "things," on the grasping and manipulation of objects, is that such a life closes the ego upon itself as though it were an end in itself, and throws it into a hopeless struggle with other perverse and hostile selves competing together for the possessions which will give them power and satisfaction. Instead of being "open to the world" such minds are in fact closed to it and their titanic efforts to build the world according to their own desires are doomed in the end by the ambiguity and destructiveness that are in them. They seem to be light, but they battle together in impenetrable moral darkness.

Buddhism and Biblical Christianity agree in their view of man's present condition. Both are aware that man is somehow not in his right relation to the world and to things in it, or rather, to be more exact, they see that man bears in himself a mysterious tendency to *falsify* that relation, and to spend a great deal of energy in justifying the false view he takes of his world and of his place in it. This falsification is what Buddhists call *Avidya*. *Avidya,* usually translated "ignorance," is the root of all evil and suffering because it places man in an equivocal, in fact impossible position. It is an invincible error concerning the very nature of reality and man himself. It is a disposition to treat the ego as an absolute and central reality and to refer all things to it as objects of desire or of repulsion. Christianity attributes this view of man and of reality to "original sin." Marcel expresses the real meaning of this blindness when he says the self creates its own obscurity by placing itself between the I and the other (who are in reality an intersubjective oneness). The story of the Fall tells us in mythical language that "original sin" is not simply a stigma arbitrarily making good pleasures seem guilty, but a basic inauthenticity, a kind of predisposition to bad faith in our understanding of ourselves and of the world. It implies a determined willfulness in trying to make things be other than they are in order that we may be able to make them subserve, at any moment, to our individual desire for pleasure or for power. But since things do not obey our arbitrary impulsions, and since we cannot make the world correspond to and confirm the image of it dictated by our needs and illusions, our willfulness is inseparable from error and from suffering. Hence, Buddhism says, deluded life itself is in a state of *Dukkha,* and every movement of desire tends to bear ultimate fruit in pain rather than lasting joy, in hate rather than love, in destruction rather than creation. (Let us note in passing that when technological skill seems in fact to give man almost absolute power in manipulating the world, this fact in no way reverses his original condition of brokenness and error but only makes it all the more obvious. We who live in the age of the H-bomb and the extermination camp have reason to reflect on this, though such reflection is a bit unpopular.)

As long as this "brokenness" of existence continues, there is no way out of the inner contradictions that it imposes upon us. If a man has a broken leg and continues to try to walk on it, he cannot help suffering. If desire itself is a kind of fracture, every movement of desire inevitably results in pain. But even the desire to end the pain of desire is a movement, and therefore causes pain. The desire to remain immobile is a movement. The desire to escape is a movement. The desire for *Nirvana* is a movement. The desire for extinction is a movement. Yet there is no way for us to be still by "imposing stillness" on the desires. In a word, desire cannot stop itself from desiring, and it must continue to move and hence to cause pain even when it seeks liberation from itself and desires its own extinction.

The ultimate Christian answer to this is typified by St. Paul: "I desire to do what is right and yet what I do is wrong. I cordially agree with the Law of God in my inner self, but I find another law in my members which contradicts the law of my mind and makes me a prisoner to sin (untruth, brokenness, wilful delusion, culpable distortion of values). . . . Unfortunate wretch that I am, who will liberate me from this living death? God, by His grace, in Christ Jesus our Lord." (Romans 7:21–25) This means of course, the Cross—death and resurrection in Christ—a life of love "in the spirit."

The Buddhist answer is in the four noble truths by which, following the teaching and experience of Buddha, man seeks to apprehend the real nature of his existence and to patiently rediscover his real roots in the true ground of all being. When man is grounded in authentic truth and love the roots of desire themselves wither, brokenness is at an end, and truth is found in the wholeness and simplicity of *Nirvana*: perfect awareness and perfect compassion. *Nirvana* is the wisdom of perfect love grounded in itself and shining through everything, meeting with no opposition. The heart of brokenness is then seen for what it was: an illusion, but a persistent and invincible illusion of the isolated ego-self, setting itself up in opposition to love, demanding that its own desire be accepted as the law of the universe, and hence suffering from the fact that by its desire it is fractured in itself and cut off from the loving wisdom in which it should be grounded.

In a word, "desire" or "craving" or "thirst" (*Tanha*)— including that thirst for continued individual existence or for nonexistence which we experience as long as we cling tenaciously to our own isolated individual ego—constitutes itself in opposition to love and being. These two are ultimately the same: the great "emptiness" of *Sunyata* which is described as emptiness only because, being completely without any limit of particularity it is also perfect fullness. When we say "fullness" we inevitably tend to imagine a "content" with a limit which defines and bounds it, and so Buddhism prefers to speak of "emptiness," not because it conceives the ultimate as mere nothingness and void, but because it is aware of the non-limitation and nondefinition of the infinite. *Nirvana* is therefore not an apprehended "content of consciousness." Hence the metaphysical concepts of Pure Being in Christian and in Buddhist philosophy—Gabriel Marcel's "mystery of Being"—tend to be much closer than has hitherto been realized. When the purity of this Buddhist metaphysic has been duly appreciated, there may be grounds for a serious discussion, with Buddhists, of the idea of God—when Absolute Reality is also Absolute Person (but never *object*).

The desire to experience *Nirvana* is, as was said before, a source of suffering, because it maintains the brokenness that cuts the subject off from the ground of his own being in *Sunyata*. This is important. Buddhism endeavors to exclude every possible trick or device by which ego-desire can have its way and salvage itself by its own power from the realm of delusion and pain.

Buddhism refuses to countenance any self-cultivation or beautification of the soul. It ruthlessly exposes any desire of enlightenment or of salvation that seeks merely the glorification of the ego and the satisfaction of its desires in a transcendent realm. It is not that this is "wrong" or "immoral" but that it is simply impossible. Ego-desire can never culminate in happiness, fulfilment and peace, because it is a fracture which cuts us off from the ground of reality in which truth and peace are found. As long as the ego seeks to "grasp" or "contain" that ground as an objective content of awareness, it will be frustrated and broken.

When Sally Donnelly in her essay calls *Nirvana* an "experience of love" we must be very careful not to misunderstand this expression. If an experience is something which one can "have" and "grasp" and "possess," if it can be an object of desire, a content of consciousness, then it is not *Nirvana*. In a sense *Nirvana* is beyond experience. Yet it is also the "highest experience" if we see it as a liberation from merely psychological limitations. The words "experience of love" must not be understood in terms of emotional fulfillment, of desire and possession, but of full realization, total awakening—a complete realization of love not merely as the emotion of a feeling subject but as the wide openness of Being itself, the realization that Pure Being is Infinite Giving, or that Absolute Emptiness is Absolute Compassion. This realization is not intellectual, not abstract, but concrete. It is, in Christ's words, "Spirit and Life." It is then not simply the awareness of a loving subject that he has love in himself, but the awareness of the Spirit of Love as the source of all that is and of all love.

Such love is beyond desire and beyond all restrictions of a desiring and self-centered self. Such love begins only when the ego renounces its claim to absolute autonomy and ceases to live in a little kingdom of desires in which it is its own end and reason for existing. Christian charity seeks to realize oneness with the other "in Christ." Buddhist compassion seeks to heal the brokenness of division and illusion and to find wholeness not in an abstract metaphysical "one" or even a pantheist immanentism but in *Nirvana*—the void which is Absolute Reality and Absolute Love. In either case the highest illumination of love is an explosion of the power of Love's evidence in which all the psychological limits of an "experiencing" subject are dissolved and what remains is the transcendent clarity of love itself, realized in the ego-less subject in a mystery beyond comprehension but not beyond consent.

For selfish desire there is and can be no fulfillment and no salvation. The only salvation, as Christ said, is found in losing oneself—that is by opening oneself to the other as another self. One does not attain to *Nirvana* by subtle and patient meditation, by experimenting with Zen *Koans,* by interminable sitting, by wheedling a secret answer out of some spiritual expert, by taming the body in various tantric ways. *Nirvana* is the extinction of desire and the full awakening that results from this extinction. It is not simply the dissolution of all ego-limits, a quasi-infinite expansion of the ego into an ocean of self-satisfaction and annihilation. This is the last and worst illusion of the ascetic who, having "crossed to the other shore," says to himself with satisfaction: "I have at last crossed to the other shore." He has, of course, crossed nothing. He is still where he was, as broken as ever. He is in the darkness of *Avidya.* He has only managed to find a pill that produces a spurious light and deadens a little of the pain.

Enlightenment is not a matter of trifling with the facticity of ordinary life and spiriting it all away. As the Buddhists say, *Nirvana* is found in the midst of the world around us, and truth is not *somewhere else.* To be here and now where we are in our "suchness" is to be in *Nirvana,* but unfortunately as long as we have "thirst" or *Tanha* we falsify our own situation and cannot realize it as *Nirvana.* As long as we are inauthentic, as long as we block and obscure the presence of what truly is, we are in delusion and we are in pain. Were we capable of a moment of perfect authenticity, of complete openness, we would see at once that *Nirvana* and *Samsara* are the same. This, I submit, implies not flight from the world, denigration of the world, repudiation of the world, but a real understanding of the value that is in the world. However, such understanding is impossible as long as one desires what the world craves and accepts the *Avidya* of the world as the source of ultimate answers.

# ZEN IN JAPANESE ART

Japanese art has traditionally been a most intimate expression of Japanese, Shinto, Confucian and Buddhist spirituality. In particular, the most contemplative paintings, ink drawings, calligraphies, and the famous "art of tea" have all been deeply impregnated with the spirit of Zen, and flourished above all in the Zen monasteries. A study of *Zen In Japanese Art**\* such as that given us by Toshimitsu Hasumi will therefore concentrate not only on the religious implications of the subject, but especially on art as a "way of spiritual experience" in Japan.

In other words, the most contemplative art forms of Japan are traditionally considered to be not simply manifestations or symbolic representations of religious belief, appropriate for use in communal worship. They are above all intimately associated with the contemplative intuition of a fundamental truth in an experience that is basically religious and even in a certain sense "mystical."

But this book of Toshimitsu Hasumi is especially interesting in that it gives us some of the fundamental aesthetic ideas of the philosopher Kitaro Nishida, whose works on aesthetics are not yet available in Western languages.

There are some differences between the disciple and the

\* *Zen In Japanese Art* by Toshimitsu Hasumi, translated from the German by John Petrie; London, Routledge and Kegan Paul, 1962; New York, Philosophical Library, 1962.

First published as a book review in *The Catholic Worker*, July-August, 1967.

master, however. Hasumi does not, for example, accept Nishida's idea of a personal God. But his view of God as the basic ground of all being and all experience, a basic ground which is apophatically termed "Nothing" or "Emptiness," is identical with that of Nishida and indeed of the Buddhist tradition. This "Nothing" is well explained by the author.

He makes clear that this manner of speaking is in no sense negativistic or pessimistic; in other words it has no relation with the *néant* of Sartre. It is the "exact opposite of the world-denying pessimistic nihilism" and is "absolutely life-affirming since Zen and Zen art regard being as the self-unfolding of the unformed Nothing."

In particular, it is the function of the beautiful to be, so to speak, an epiphany of the Absolute and formless Void which is God. It is an embodiment of the Absolute mediated through the personality of the artist, or perhaps better his "spirit" and his contemplative experience.

The contribution of Zen to art is then a profound spiritual dimension and transforms art into an essentially contemplative experience in which it awakens "the primal consciousness hidden within us and which makes possible any spiritual activity."

In this traditional Japanese concept of art, we find no divorce between art and life or art and spirituality. On the contrary, under the unifying power of the Zen discipline and intuition, art, life and spiritual experience are all brought together and inseparably fused. Nowhere is this more clearly and more beautifully shown than in the "art of tea." The pages devoted to this by the author are of superlative interest for monks everywhere, for they depict a monastic and contemplative style of life in which art, spiritual experience and communal, personal relationships enter together into an expression of God in His world. Far from being a stilted social formality, as some Western observers may have imagined, the "tea ceremony" is in reality a deeply spiritual, one might be tempted to say "liturgical," expression of art and faith. In the tea ceremony everything is important, everything is guided by traditional rules, yet within this traditional framework there is also room for originality, spontaneity and spiritual freedom. The spirit of the tea ceremony is found in the basic norms which govern it: Harmony, Respect, Purity (of heart) and Stillness (in the sense of *quies* and *hesychia*). But to make this spirit more evident we can say that it is the same sort of spirit manifested in the simplicity of twelfth-century Cistercian architecture at Fontenay or Le Thoronet: an inward joy in poverty and simplicity, for which the untranslatable Japanese term is *Wabi*. Hasumi describes it in an arresting phase as "an inwardly echoing aesthetic poverty." Surely this is a most important concept for those of us who are struggling to recover something of the contemplative and spiritual concept of simplicity and poverty which are essential to the Cistercian way of life. The "Stillness" and the "listening" in which "we reverence the poverty of man, the harmony of the world, and the incompleteness of nature" opens into a deep awareness "of the eternal present in which all ideals flow together in the 'Nothing'." This expression of the contemplative experience may perhaps disconcert the Christian reader who is not familiar with the apophatic tradition in his own spiritual heritage. It is not by any means mere quietistic and inert vacuity. Nor is it a negation, a blacking out of human reality. On the contrary, "The souls of the guest and host surrender their personal selves and become united with each other. In the reality of this sphere the antinomy between soul and body is abolished and grows into harmonious unity. Man himself has now become a soul in the form of art. The separateness of existence and being no longer exists, the soul is freed from the body and man feels himself a solitary being full of meaning and close to the essence of things." This description, which is impressionistic and poetic rather than scientifically exact, should serve to give some idea of the "art of tea" as a deeply influential spiritual force in Japanese tradition.

In conclusion, we may remark that the author is conscious of similarities and contrasts between the Buddhist and Christian traditions, and he makes a statement which could be enlightening to those who are beginning to be interested in a possible dialogue between the two religions.

"Christianity is a manifestation of the Incarnation of God, whereas Zen is intensive, inward enlightening of the divine being which the Japanese has apprehended as Nothing, and which must be supplemented, uplifted and completed by means of the manifestation of the Incarnation." Surely this is a very generous and perceptive statement of what the Buddhist might expect from his Christian brethren.

# APPENDIX: IS BUDDHISM LIFE-DENYING?

Without engaging in a detailed argument, let me simply quote a few texts with a minimum of necessary comment.

It is usually thought in the West that a Buddhist simply turns away from the world and other people as "unreal" and cultivates meditation in order to enter a trance and eventually a complete negative state of *Nirvana*. But Buddhist "mindfulness," far from being contemptuous of life, is extremely solicitious for all life. It has two aspects: one, the penetration of the meaning and reality of suffering by meditation, and two, the protection of all beings against suffering by nonviolence and compassion.

The following quotation from the *Samyutta Nikaya* shows how both meditation and nonviolence are directed toward the protection of life in oneself and in others, while at the same time uniting compassion and detachment, insight and pity. Insight attained by meditation is not contemptuous of life but highly respectful of it. Without such insight, there can be no real respect for life. Without such insight it is easy to multiply fine words about being "life-affirming" and about love of others: but one destroys them nevertheless.

> "I will protect myself" thus the Foundations of Mindfulness have to be cultivated. "I will protect others" thus the Foundations of Mindfulness have to be cultivated. *By protecting oneself one is protecting others; by protecting others one is protecting oneself.*
>
> And how does one by protecting oneself protect others? By repeated practice, by meditative culture of mind and by frequent occupation with it.

And how does one by protecting others protect oneself? By patience, by a non-violent life, by loving-kindness and compassion. (Nyanaponika Thera, *The Heart of Buddhist Meditation*, Colombo, 1956, p. 57)

But is the Buddhist meditation on suffering, in order to attain deliverance from ignorance and the "round of birth and death," not morbid, masochistic? Does it not instill a contempt for life itself? Suzuki says:

"The value of human life lies in the fact of suffering, for where there is no suffering, no consciousness of karmic bondage, there will be no power of attaining spiritual experience and thereby reaching the field of non-distinction. *Unless we agree to suffer we cannot be free from suffering.*" (*Essence of Buddhism*, p. 13)

Contrast this with the triviality and futility of a superficially "life-affirming" optimism which seeks only to escape suffering in what Pascal called "diversion" or "distraction"—an attempt to avoid facing suffering as a reality inseparable from life itself!

Does Buddhism simply seek to escape from life? Lama Angarika Govinda says:

"(The way of *Mahayana*) is not a way of running away from the world but of overcoming it through growing knowledge (*Prajna*) through active love (*Maitri*) towards ones fellow beings, through inner participation in the joys and sufferings of others (*Karuna, Mudita*) and through equanimity (*Upeksa*) with regard to one's own weal and woe." (*Foundations of Tibetan Mysticism*, p. 40)

Does Buddhism preach a purely negative contempt for the world? The same author explains the Buddhist position as follows:

"(The world) is neither condemned in its totality nor torn into irreconcilable opposites, but a bridge is shown which leads from the ordinary temporal world of sense perception to the realm of timeless knowledge—a way which leads beyond the world not through contempt or negation but through purification and sublimation of the conditions and qualities of our present existence." (Govinda, *Foundations*, p. 108)

Does Buddhist meditation deny the body entirely and seek to pass over into a realm of purely spiritual abstraction? Quite the contrary. The body plays a most important part in Buddhist meditation, in fact in no other meditation discipline is the body so important. Instead of eliminating, or trying to eliminate, all body-consciousness, Buddhist meditation is keenly aware of the body. In order to master the mind, Buddhist meditation seeks first of all to master the body. "If the body is unmastered (by mediation) the mind will be unmastered; if the body is mastered, the mind is mastered.

"Since mental processes will become clear only to one who has grasped the corporeal with full clarity, any endeavour in grasping the mental processes should be made only through grasping the corporeal, not otherwise." (Nyanaponika Thera, *The Heart*, p. 78)

PART TWO

# WISDOM IN EMPTINESS

*A Dialogue by Daisetz T. Suzuki and Thomas Merton*

*Prefatory Note:*

In the spring of 1959, after the completion of some translations from the *Verba Seniorum,* which has been published by New Directions under the title of *The Wisdom of the Desert,* it was decided to send the text of the translation to Daisetz Suzuki, one of the most prominent Oriental scholars and contemplatives of our day. It was felt that the *Verba,* in their austere simplicity, bore a remarkable resemblance to some of the stories told of the Japanese Zen Masters, and that Dr. Suzuki would probably be interested in them for that reason. He received with pleasure the suggestion to engage in a dialogue about the "wisdom" of the Desert Fathers and of the Zen Masters.

It was felt that an exchange of views would contribute something to the mutual understanding of East and West, and that it might be quite enlightening to confront the Egyptian monks of the fourth and fifth centuries with Chinese and Japanese monks of a slightly later date. (Zen* was beginning in China about the end of the great age of the Desert Fathers in Egypt.) Zen Buddhism is the object of considerable interest in the West today, largely because of its paradoxical and highly existential simplicity, which stands as a kind of challenge to

---

* Zen is the Japanese term for the Chinese *Ch'an,* from the Sanscrit *Dhyana.* For the sake of convenience, I use "Zen" when referring to *Ch'an.*

the complicated and verbalistic ideologies which have become substitutes for religion, philosophy and spirituality in the Western world.

There are countless Zen stories that almost exactly reproduce the *Verba Seniorum*—incidents which are obviously likely to occur wherever men seek and realize the same kind of poverty, solitude and emptiness. For instance, there is always the problem of the robber—and the solution of the humble monk who not only permits the robber to take everything but even runs after him with the object he has overlooked.

As Dr. Suzuki makes clear in his analysis of "innocence," this is really something beyond the level of problem-and-solution. When the monk acts in the primitive emptiness and innocence which the Zen-man calls "suchness" and the Christian calls "purity of heart" or "perfect charity"—then the problem does not even arise. As St. Paul says, "Against such there is no law." He might as well have said *For* such there is no law. It works both ways—the law has for them neither advantages nor disadvantages. They neither appeal to it in their own defense nor suffer from its effects. They are "beyond the law."

But this idea is often misunderstood and even more often misapplied. Wherever one comes face to face with a simple and mystical spirituality, the same difficulties always afflict the ordinary student who sees it from the outside. The same questions clamor for an answer, the same accusations demand to be refuted. There are always those who mistake the "liberty of the sons of God" for the license of those who are slaves of illusion and of self-will.

In the East and West alike, contemplatives are always being reproached for idleness, escapism, quietism, misanthropy and a hundred other sins. And more often than not they are accused of despising ordinary ways of ethical and ascetic discipline and of throwing morality and politics completely out of the window. This reproach of antinomianism is frequently leveled against the Zen-man who has a way of being extremely paradoxical, and even shocking, like the "fool for Christ" once so common in Russian Christendom.

As a matter of fact, Zen is at present most fashionable in America among those who are least concerned with moral discipline. Zen has, indeed, become for us a symbol of moral revolt. It is true, the Zen-man's contempt for conventional and formalistic social custom is a healthy phenomenon, but it is healthy only because it presupposes a spiritual liberty based on freedom from passion, egotism and self-delusion. A pseudo-Zen attitude which seeks to justify a complete moral collapse with a few rationalizations based on the Zen Masters is only another form of bourgeois self-deception. It is not an expression of healthy revolt, but only another aspect of the same lifeless and inert conventionalism against which it appears to be protesting.

If Dr. Suzuki has taken up the ethical aspect of Zen, it is not because of anything in the Desert Fathers but rather because another, anonymous, interlocutor found his way into the dialogue. In the summer of 1959 Dr. Suzuki attended the East–West conference of philosophers in Hawaii and had to meet with this ethical objection to Zen. He has made his answer the starting point of his essay on the Desert Fathers. In doing so, he has not strayed from the subject, but entered directly into its very heart. And thus he has been able to make some very astute observations on the spirituality of the desert, with its hazards and limitations.

The theme Dr. Suzuki has here stressed is one that is not altogether unfamiliar in the West today. It is the question of "science and wisdom" which has been frequently discussed by Thomists like Maritain and Gilson, though in more technical and scholastic contexts. This is an ancient and traditional theme in Patristic theology, and one which played a central part in the spirituality of St. Augustine and all his followers, as well as in the writings of the Greek Fathers. It was, as a matter of fact, very important to the Alexandrian writers who provided the intellectual basis for the spirituality of the desert.

But what is most fascinating about this particular essay is that the Zen concepts of "emptiness," "discrimination," etc., are evaluated in terms of the Biblical story of the Fall of Adam. Dr. Suzuki comes out with an equation of "Knowledge" with "Ignorance" and true Wisdom with Innocence, emptiness, or "Suchness." This is precisely the same type of approach as was taken by the early Christian Fathers. There are of course significant differences, but the similarities are much greater than the differences. And it is in order to point this out that I have added my own essay on the "Recovery of Paradise"—meaning the recovery of that "purity" or "emptiness" which for the early Fathers was union with the divine light, not considered as an "object" or "thing" but as the "divine poverty" which enriches and transforms us in its own innocence. The Recovery of Paradise is the discovery of the "Kingdom of God within us," to use the Gospel expression in the sense in which it has always been applied by the Christian mystics. It is the recovery of man's lost likeness to God in pure, undivided simplicity.

It is hoped that this will bring out still more the extraordinary significance of Dr. Suzuki's study, which is, without doubt, one of the most cogent of his recent essays, at least for the Christian reader. It is surely striking that this Oriental writer, in undertaking to discuss the Fathers of the Desert, should take as his main theme the contrast between the "innocence" of Adam in Paradise (with its attendant "wisdom"—*sapientia*—*Prajna*) and the "knowledge" of good-and-evil, the *scientia*, which resulted from the Fall and, in a sense, constituted it. It is certainly a matter of very great significance that Dr. Suzuki should choose, as the best and most obvious common ground for a dialogue between East and West, not the exterior surface of the Desert spirituality (with its ascetic practices and its meditative solitude) but the most primitive and most archetypal fact of all Judaeo-Christian spirituality: the narrative of the Creation and Fall of man in the Book of Genesis.

KNOWLEDGE AND INNOCENCE

*by Daisetz T. Suzuki*

I

When I speak about Zen to the Western audience, mostly brought up in Christian tradition, the first question generally asked is: "What is the Zen concept of morality? If Zen claims to be above all moral values, what does it teach us ordinary mortals?"

If I understand Christianity correctly, it derives the moral authority from God who is the giver of the Decalogue, and we are told that if we violate it in any way we shall be punished and thrown into everlasting fire. It is for this reason that atheists are regarded as dangerous people, for they have no God and are no respecters of moral codes. The Zen-man, too, having no God that corresponds to the analogical Christian God, but who talks of going beyond the dualism of good and evil, of right and wrong, of life and death, of truth and falsehood, will most likely be a subject of suspicion. The idea of social values deeply ingrained in Western minds is intimately connected with religion so that they are led to think religion and ethics are one and the same, and that religion can ill-afford to relegate ethics to a position of secondary importance. But Zen seems to do this, hence the following question:[1] "Dr. Suzuki writes: 'All the moral values and social practice come out of this life of Suchness which is Emptiness.' If this is so, then 'good' and 'evil' are secondary differentiations. What differentiates them and how do I know what is 'good' other than 'evil'? In other words, can I—and if so, how can I—derive an ethics from the ontology of Zen Buddhism?"

We are all social beings and ethics is our concern with social life. The Zen-man too cannot live outside society. He cannot ignore the ethical values. Only, he wants to have the heart thoroughly cleansed of all impurities issuing from "Knowledge"[2] which we acquired by eating the fruit of the forbidden tree. When we return to the state of "innocence,"[2] anything we do is good. St. Augustine says, "Love God and do as you will." The Buddhist idea of *Anabhoga-Carya*[3] corresponds to Innocence. When Knowledge is awakened in the Garden of Eden where Innocence prevails, the differentiation of good and evil takes place. In the same way, out of the

[1] This question was submitted to me by one of the members taking part in the Third East–West Philosophers' Conference at the University of Hawaii, June–July, 1959. It was based on the paper I contributed to this Conference. My answer, which follows here, requires further elaboration for which I have no time just now. It involves my view on the Judaeo-Christian creation account.

[2] Throughout this paper, "Innocence" is to be taken as the state of mind in which inhabitants of the Garden of Eden used to live around the tree of life, with eyes not opened, all naked, not ashamed, with no knowledge of good and evil; whereas "Knowledge" refers to everything opposite of "Innocence," especially a pair of discriminating eyes widely opened to good and evil.

[3] See D.T. Suzuki, (trans.) *Lankavatara Sutra* (London: Routledge & Kegan Paul), 1957, pp. 32, 43, 89, etc., where the term is translated "effortless" or "no striving" act.

Emptiness of the Mind a thought mysteriously rises and we have the world of multiplicities.[4]

The Judaeo-Christian idea of Innocence is the moral interpretation of the Buddhist doctrine of Emptiness which is metaphysical, whereast the Judaeo-Christian idea of Knowledge epistemologically corresponds to the Buddhist notion of Ignorance though superficially Ignorance is the opposite of Knowledge. Buddhist philosophy considers discrimination of any kind—moral or metaphysical—the product of Ignorance which obscures the original light of Suchness which is Emptiness. But this does not mean that the whole world is to be done away with because of its being the outcome of Ignorance. It is the same with Knowledge, for Knowledge is the outcome of our having lost Innocence by eating the forbidden fruit. But no Christians or Jews, as far as I am aware, have ever attempted to get rid of Knowledge in order to regain Paradise whereby they might enjoy the bliss of Innocence to its full extent as they originally did.

What we are to realize, then, is the meaning of "Knowledge" and "Innocence," that is to say, to have a thoroughly penetrating insight into the relationship between the two opposing concepts—Innocence and Original Light on the one side, and Knowledge and Ignorance on the other. In one sense they seem to be irreducibly contradictory, but in another sense they are complementary. As far as our human way of thinking is concerned, we cannot have them both at the same time, but our actual life consists in the one supporting the other, or better, that they are inseparably co-operating.

The so-called opposition between Innocence and Knowledge or between Ignorance and the Original Light is not the kind of opposition we see between black and white, good

[4] D.T. Suzuki (trans.) *Asvaghosa's Awakening of Faith* (Chicago: Open Court Publishing Co.), 1900, pp. 78-9.

and evil, right and wrong, to be and not to be, or to have and not to have. The opposition is, as it were, between container and the contained, between the background and the stage, between the field and the players moving on it. The good and the evil play their opposing parts on the field which remains neutral and indifferent and "open" or "empty." It is like rain that falls on the just and on the unjust. It is like the sun rising on the good and on the evil, on your foes and on your friends. In a way, the sun is innocent and perfect, as is the rain. But man who has lost Innocence and acquired Knowledge differentiates just from unjust, good from evil, right from wrong, foes from friends. He is, therefore, no longer innocent and perfect, but highly "morally" conscious. To be "moral" apparently means the loss of Innocence, and the acquirement of Knowledge, religiously speaking, is not always conducive to our inner happiness or divine blessings. The outcome of "moral" responsibility may sometimes lead to the violation of civil laws. The outcome of the "great hermit's" inner goodness in releasing the robbers from jail (Cf. *Wisdom of the Desert* 37)[5] may be far from being desirable. Innocence and Knowledge must be kept well balanced. To do this Knowledge must be disciplined and at the same time the value of Innocence must be appraised in its proper relation to Knowledge.

[5] "There was once a great hermit in the mountains and he was attacked by robbers. But his cries aroused the other hermits in the neighborhood, and they ran together and captured the robbers. These they sent under guard to the town and the judge put them in jail. But then the brothers were very ashamed and sad because, on their account, the robbers had been turned over to the judge. They went to Abbot Poemen and told him all about it. And the elder wrote to the hermit saying: Remember who carried out the first betrayal, and you will learn the reason for the second. Unless you had first been betrayed by your own inward thoughts, you would never have ended by turning those men over to the judge. The hermit, touched by these words, got up at once and went into the city and broke open the jail, letting out the robbers and freeing them from torture."—*The Wisdom of The Desert, XXXVII.*

In the *Dhammapada* (verse 183) we have:

Not to do anything that is evil,
To do all that is good,
To thoroughly purify the heart:
This is the teaching of Buddhas.

The first two lines refer to Knowledge, whereas the third is the state of Innocence. "To purify" means "to purge," "to empty" all that pollutes the mind. The pollution comes from the egocentric consciousness which is Ignorance or Knowledge which distinguishes good from evil, ego from nonego. Metaphysically speaking, it is the mind that realizes the truth of Emptiness, and when this is done it knows that there is no self, no ego, no *Atman* that will pollute the mind, which is a state of zero. It is out of this zero that all good is performed and all evil is avoided. The zero I speak of is not a mathematical symbol. It is the infinite—a storehouse or womb (*Garbha*) of all possible good or values.

$$\text{zero} = \text{infinity, and infinity} = \text{zero.}$$

The double equation is to be understood not only statically but dynamically. It takes place between being and becoming. For they are not contradicting ideas. Emptiness is not sheer emptiness or passivity or Innocence. It is and at the same time it is not. It is Being, it is Becoming. It is Knowledge and Innocence. The Knowledge to do good and not to do evil is not enough; it must come out of Innocence, where Innocence is Knowledge and Knowledge is Innocence.

The "great hermit" is guilty of not realizing Emptiness, that is, Innocence, and Abbot Poemen commits an error in applying Innocence minus Knowledge to the affairs of the world. The robbers are to be consigned to prison, for the community will suffer; as long as they are outlaws they must be deprived of their liberty—this is the way of the world in which we carry on our business of earning bread by hard, honest labor. Our business is possible only by living in the world of Knowledge, because where Innocence prevails there is no need for our laboring: "All that is needed for our existence is given freely by God." As long as we live a communal life, all kinds of law are to be observed. We are sinners, that is, we are knowers not only individually but collectively, communally, socially. The robbers are to be confined in prison. As spiritual beings we are to strive after Innocence, Emptiness, enlightenment and a prayerful life. "The great hermit" must lead a life of penance and prayer but not interfere with the laws of the land that regulate our secular life. Where secular life goes on, Knowledge predominates, and hard and honest labor is an absolute necessity, and, further, each individual is entitled to the fruit of his work. "The great hermit" has no right to release the robbers, thereby threatening the peace of law-abiding fellow beings. When Knowledge is not properly exercised, strange, irrational phenomena will take place. The hermit is no doubt a good social member and he means no harm to any of his fellow beings; the robbers are those bent on disturbing the peace of the community to which they belong. They must be kept away from the community. The hermit deserves to be imprisoned for having violated the law by freeing the antisocial members. The good man is punished, while the bad men roam about free and unhampered, annoying peace-loving citizens. This, I am sure, is far from the hermit's aspirations.


II

The metaphysical concept of Emptiness is convertible in economic terms into poverty, being poor, having nothing:

"Blessed are those who are poor in spirit." Eckhart defines, "He is a poor man who wants nothing, knows nothing, and has nothing." This is possible when a man is empty of "self and all things," when the mind is thoroughly purified of Knowledge or Ignorance, which we have after the loss of Innocence. In other words, to gain Innocence again is to be poor. What strikes one as somewhat strange is Eckhart representing a poor man as knowing nothing. This is a very significant statement. The beginning of Knowledge is when the mind is filled with all kinds of defiled thought among which the worst is "self." For all evils and defilements start from our attachment to it. As Buddhists would say, the realization of Emptiness is no more, no less than seeing into the nonexistence of a thingish ego-substance. This is the greatest stumbling block in our spiritual discipline, which, in actuality, consists not in getting rid of the self but in realizing the fact that there is no such existence from the first. The realization means being "poor" in spirit. "Being poor" does not mean "becoming poor;" "being poor" means to be from the very beginning not in possession of anything and not giving away what one has. Nothing to gain, nothing to lose; nothing to give, nothing to take; to be just so, and yet to be rich in inexhaustible possibilities—this is to be "poor" in its most proper and characteristic sense of the word, this is what all religious experiences tells us. To be absolutely nothing is to be everything. When one is in possession of something, that something will keep all other somethings from coming in.

In this respect, Eckhart had a wonderful insight into the nature of what he calls *die eigentlichste Armut*. We are generally apt to imagine that when the mind or heart is emptied of "self and all things" a room is left ready for God to enter and occupy it. This is a great error. The very thought, even the slightest, of making room for something is a hindrance as monstrous as the mountain. A monk came to Ummon, the great Zen Master (who died in 949), and said, "When a man has not one thought occupying his consciousness, what fault has he?" Ummon roared, "Mount Sumeru!" Another Zen Master,[6] Kyogen Chikan, has his song of poverty:

Last year's poverty was not yet perfect;
This year's poverty is absolute.
In last year's poverty there was room for the head of a gimlet;
This year's poverty has let the gimlet itself disappear.

Eckhart's statement corresponding to Kyogen's runs in this wise, where he is typically Christian:

"If it is the case that a man is emptied of things, creatures, himself and God, and if still God could find a place in him to act, then we say: as long as that (place) exists, this man is not poor with the most intimate poverty (*eigentlichste Armut*). For God does not intend that man shall have a place reserved for him to work in, since the true poverty of spirit requires that man shall be emptied of God and all his works, so that if God wants to act in the soul, he himself must be the place in which he acts—and that he would like to do. For if God once found a person as poor as this, he would take the responsibility of his own action and would himself be the scene of action, for God is one who acts within himself. It is here, in this poverty, that man regains the eternal being that once he was, now is, and evermore shall be."

As I interpret Eckhart, God is at once the place where He works and the work itself. The place is zero or "Emptiness as Being," whereas the work which is carried on in the zero-place is infinity or "Emptiness as Becoming." When the double equation, zero = infinity and infinity = zero, is realized, we

[6] Disciple of Isan Reiyu, 770-853.

have the *eigentlichste Armut,* or the essence of poverty. Being is becoming and becoming is being. When the one is separated from the other, we have a poverty crooked and limping. Perfect poverty is recovered only when perfect emptiness is perfect fullness.

When a monk[7] has anything to loan and when he feels anxious to have it returned, he is not yet poor, he is not yet perfectly empty. Some years ago when I was reading stories of pious Buddhists I remember having come across one of a farmer. One evening he heard some noise in the garden. He noticed a young man of the village atop a tree stealing his fruit. Quietly, he went to the shed where he kept his ladder and took it under the tree so that the intruder might safely make his descent. He went back to his bed unnoticed. The farmer's heart, emptied of self and possession, could not think of anything else but the danger that might befall the young village delinquent.


III

There is a set of what may be called fundamental moral virtues of perfection in Mahayana Buddhism known as the Six Paramita. Followers of the Mahayana are expected to exert themselves to practice these virtues in their daily life. They are: (1) *Dana,* "giving"; (2) *Sila,* "observing the precepts"; (3) *Virya,* "spirit of manhood"; (4) *Ksanti,* "humility"

[7] "A certain brother asked of an elder, saying: If a brother owes me a little money, do you think I should ask him to pay me back? The elder said to him: Ask him for it once only, and with humility. The brother said: Suppose I ask him once and he doesn't give me anything, what should I do? Then the elder said: Don't ask him any more. The brother said again: But what can I do, I cannot get rid of my anxieties about it, unless I go and ask him? The elder said to him: Forget your anxieties. The important thing is not to sadden your brother, for you are a monk."
—*The Wisdom of The Desert,* XVCVIII.

or "patience"; (5) *Dhyana,* "meditation"; and (6) *Prajna,* "transcendental wisdom," which is an intuition of the highest order.

I am not going to explain each item of the six virtues here. All that I can try is to call the attention of our readers to the order in which they are set. First comes *Dana,* to give, and the last is *Prajna,* which is a kind of spiritual insight into the truth of Emptiness. The Buddhist life starts with "giving" and ends in *Prajna.* But, in reality, the ending is the beginning and the beginning is the ending; the Paramita moves in a circle with no beginning and no ending. The giving is possible only when there is Emptiness, and Emptiness is attainable only when the giving is unconditionally carried out—which is *die eigentlichste Armut* of Eckhart.

As *Prajna* has been frequently the subject of discussion, I shall limit myself to the exposition of *Dana,* giving. It does not just mean giving in charity or otherwise something material in one's possession as is usually understood when we talk of "giving." It means anything going out of oneself, disseminating knowledge, helping people in difficulties of all kinds, creating arts, promoting industry or social welfare, sacrificing one's life for a worthy cause and so on. But this, however noble, Buddhist philosophers would say, is not enough as long as a man harbors the idea of giving in one sense or another. The genuine giving consists in not cherishing any thought of anything going out of one's hands and being received by anybody else; that is to say, in the giving there must not be any thought of a giver or a receiver, and of an object going through this transaction. When the giving goes on thus in Emptiness, it is the deed of *Dana,* the first Paramita, directly flowing out of *Prajna,* the final Paramita. According to Eckhart's definition, as was quoted above, it is poverty in its genuine sense. In another place he is more concrete by referring to examples:

> "St. Peter said, "We have left all things." St. James said, "We have given up all things." St. John said, "We have nothing left." Whereupon Brother Eckhart asks, When do we leave all things? When we leave everything conceivable, everything expressible, everything audible, everything visible, then and then only we give up all things. When in this sense we give up all, we grow aflood with light, passing bright with God."

Kyogen the Zen Master says: "This year's poverty has let the gimlet itself disappear." This is symbolical. In point of fact it means that one is dead to oneself, corresponding to:

> *Visankharagatam cittam,*
> Gone to dissolution is the mind,
> *Tanhanam khayam ajjhaga.*[8]
> The cravings have come to an end.

This is part of the verse ascribed to Buddha when he attained the supreme enlightenment, and it is known as the "Hymn of Victory." The gimlet is "dissolved," the body is "dissolved," the mind is "dissolved," all is "dissolved"—is this not Emptiness? In other words, it is the perfect state of poverty. Eckhart quotes St. Gregory, "No one gets so much of God as the man who is thoroughly dead." I do not know exactly in what sense St. Gregory uses the word "dead." But the word is most significant if it is understood in reference to Bunan Zenji's[9] poem:

> While alive, be dead,
> Thoroughly dead—
> All is good then,
> Whatever you may do.

[8] The *Dhammapada*, verse 154.
[9] Lived 1603-76.

Emptiness, poverty, death or dissolution—they are all realized when one goes through the experiences of "breaking-through" which is nothing else but "enlightenment" (*Sambodhi*). Let me quote a little more from Eckhart:

> "In my breaking-through, . . . I transcend all creatures and am neither God nor creature: I am that I was and I shall remain now and forever. Then I receive an impulse (*Aufschwung*) which carries me above all angels. In this impulse I conceive such passing riches that I am not content with God as being God, as being all his godly works, for in this breaking-through I find that God and I are both the same. . . ."

I do not know how my Christian readers would take these statements, but from the Buddhist point of view one reservation is needed, which is: However transcendental and above all forms of conditionality this experience itself of "breaking-through" may be, we are liable to formulate a distorted interpretation of the experience. The Zen Master therefore will tell us to transcend or "to cast away" the experience itself. To be absolutely naked, to go even beyond the receiving of "an impulse" of whatever nature, to be perfectly free from every possible remnant of the trappings we have put on ourselves ever since the acquisition of Knowledge—this is the goal of the Zen training. Then and only then do we find ourselves again to be the ordinary Toms, Dicks and Harrys we had been all along. It was Joshu, one of the greatest masters of the T'ang, who confessed something like this: "I get up early in the morning and look at myself—how poorly dressed I am! My upper robe is nearly reduced to tatters, my surplice somewhat holding its shape. My head is covered with dirt and ashes. When I first started the study of Zen, I dreamed of becoming a fine imposing clergyman. But I never imagined that I should be living in this tottering shanty and eating scanty meals. After all, I am a poor beggar-monk."

A monk came to this man and asked, "When a man comes to you free of all possible possession, how would this do?" Joshu answered, "Throw it away!"

Still another came and asked, "Who is Buddha?" Joshu retorted instantly, "Who are you?"

An old woman visited Joshu saying, "I am a woman, who according to Buddhism lives under five obstructions;[10] how can I surpass them? Joshu advised her: "Pray that all beings may be born in Paradise, but as to myself, let me forever remain in this ocean of tribulations."

We may enumerate a number of virtues to be pursued by monks, Buddhist or Christian, such as poverty, tribulation, discretion, obedience, humility, not-judging-others, meditation, silence, simplicity and some other qualities, but the most fundamental one is in my opinion poverty. Poverty corresponds ontologically to Emptiness and psychologically to self-lessness or Innocence. The life we used to enjoy in the Garden of Eden symbolizes Innocence. How to regain (or perhaps better how to recognize that we already possess) this primitive-mindedness in the midst of industrialization and the universal propagandism of "an easy life" is the grave question given to us modern men for successful solution. How to actualize the transcendental wisdom of *Prajna* in a world where the growth of Knowledge is everywhere encouraged in a thousand and one ways? A solution is imperatively demanded of us in a most poignant manner. The day of the Desert Fathers is forever gone and we are waiting for a new sun to rise above the horizon of egotism and sordidness in every sense.

---

[10] A woman is said not to be qualified to be: (1) Mahabrahman, "supreme spirit," (2) Sakrendra, "king of the heavens," (3) Mara, "evil one," (4) Cakravartin, "great lord" and (5) Buddha.

*by Thomas Merton*

I

One of Dostoevski's "saints," the Staretz Zosima who speaks as a typical witness to the tradition of the Greek and Russian Church, makes an astonishing declaration. He says: "We do not understand that life is paradise, for it suffices only to wish to understand it, and at once paradise will appear in front of us in its beauty." Taken in the context of the *Brothers Karamazov,* against the background of violence, blasphemy and murder which fill the book, this is indeed an astonishing statement. Was Zosima perfectly serious? Or was he simply a deluded idiot, dreaming the frantic dreams inspired by the "opium of the people"?

Whatever the modern reader may think of this claim, it was certainly something basic to primitive Christianity. Modern studies of the Fathers have revealed beyond question that one of the main motives that impelled men to embrace the "angelic life" (*bios angelikos*) of solitude and poverty in the desert was precisely the hope that by so doing they might return to paradise.

Now this concept must be properly and accurately understood. Paradise is not "heaven." Paradise is a state, or indeed a place, on earth. Paradise belongs more properly to the present than to the future life. In some sense it belongs to both. It is the state in which man was originally created to live on earth. It is also conceived as a kind of antechamber to heaven after death—as for instance at the end of Dante's *Purgatorio.* Christ, dying on the cross, said to the good thief at His side: "This day thou shalt be with me *in Paradise,"* and it was clear that this did not mean, and could not have meant, heaven.

We must not imagine Paradise as a place of ease and

sensual pleasure. It is a state of peace and rest, by all means. But what the Desert Fathers sought when they believed they could find "paradise" in the desert, was the lost innocence, the emptiness and purity of heart which had belonged to Adam and Eve in Eden. Evidently they could not have expected to find beautiful trees and gardens in the waterless desert, burned by the sun. Obviously they did not expect to find a place, among the fiery rocks and caves, where they could recline at ease in shady groves, by cool running water. What they sought was paradise within themselves, or rather above and beyond themselves. They sought paradise in the recovery of that "unity" which had been shattered by the "knowledge of good and evil."

In the beginning, Adam was "one man." The Fall had divided him into "a multitude." Christ had restored man to unity in Himself. The Mystical Christ was the "New Adam" and in Him all men could return to unity, to innocence, to purity, and become "one man." *Omnes in Christo unum.* This meant, of course, living not by one's own will, one's own ego, one's own limited and selfish spirit, but being "one spirit" with Christ. "Those who are united to the Lord," says St. Paul, "are *one spirit."* Union with Christ means unity in Christ, so that each one who is in Christ can say, with Paul: "It is now not I that live but Christ that lives in me." It is the same Christ who lives in all. The individual has "died" with Christ to his "old man," his exterior, egotistical self, and "risen" in Christ to the new man, a selfless and divine being, who is the one Christ, the same who is "all in all."

The great difference between Christianity and Buddhism arises at this juncture. From the metaphysical point of view, Buddhism seems to take "emptiness" as a complete negation of all personality, whereas Christianity finds in purity of heart and "unity of spirit," a supreme and transcendent fulfillment of personality. This is an extremely complex and difficult question which I am not prepared to discuss. But it seems to me that most discussions on the point, up to now, have been completely equivocal. Very often, on the Christian side, we identify "personality" with the illusory and exterior ego-self, which is certainly not the true Christian "person." On the Buddhist side there seems to be no positive idea of personality at all: it is a value which seems to be completely missing from Buddhist thought. Yet it is certainly not absent from Buddhist practice, as is evident from Dr. Suzuki's remark that at the end of Zen training, when one has become "absolutely naked," one finds himself to be the ordinary "Tom, Dick or Harry" that he has been all along. This seems to me, in practice, to correspond to the idea that a Christian can lose his "old man" and find his true self "in Christ." The main difference is that the language and practice of Zen are much more radical, austere and ruthless, and that where the Zen-man says "emptiness" he leaves no room for any image or concept to confuse the real issue. The Christian treatment of the subject makes free use of richly metaphorical expressions and of concrete imagery, but we must take care to penetrate beyond the exterior surface and reach the inner depths. In any case the "death of the old man" is not the destruction of personality but the dissipation of an illusion, and the discovery of the new man is the realization of what was there all along, at least as a radical possibility, by reason of the fact that man is the image of God.

These Christian themes of "life in Christ" and "unity in Christ" are familiar enough, but one feels that today they are not understood in all their spiritual depth. Their mystical implications are seldom explored. We dwell rather, with much greater interest, on their social, economic and ethical implications. I wonder if what Dr. Suzuki had said about "emptiness" ought not to help us to go deeper than we usually do into this doctrine of our mystical unity and purity in Christ. Anyone who has read St. John of the Cross and his doctrine of "night" will be inclined to ask the same question. If we are to die to ourselves and live "in Christ," does that not mean that we must somehow find ourselves "dead" and "empty" with regard to our old self? If we are to be moved in all things by the grace of Christ should we not in some sense realize this as action out-of-emptiness, springing from the mystery of the pure freedom which is "divine love," rather than as something produced in and with our egotistical, exterior self, springing from our desires and referred to our own spiritual interest?

St. John of the Cross compares man to a window through which the light of God is shining. If the windowpane is clean of every stain, it is completely transparent, we do not see it at all: it is "empty" and nothing is seen but the light. But if a man bears in himself the stains of spiritual egotism and preoccupation with his illusory and exterior self, even in "good things," then the windowpane itself is clearly seen by reason of the stains that are on it. Hence if a man can be rid of the stains and dust produced within him by his fixation upon what is good and bad in reference to himself, he will be transformed in God and will be "one with God." In the terms of St. John of the Cross:

> "In thus allowing God to work in it, the soul (having rid itself of every mist and stain of creatures, which consists in having its will perfectly united with that of God, for to love is to labour to detach and strip itself for God's sake of all that is not God) is at once illumined and transformed in God, and God communicates to it His supernatural being in such wise that the soul appears to be God Himself, and has all that God Himself has. . . . All the things of God and the soul are one in participant

transformation; and the soul seems to be God rather than the soul, and is indeed God by participation." (St. John of the Cross, *Ascent to Mount Carmel*, II, v. Peers trans. vol. i, p. 82)

This, as we shall see, is what the Fathers called "purity of heart," and it corresponds to a recovery of the innocence of Adam in Paradise. The many stories of the Desert Fathers in which they are shown to have exercised an extraordinary control over wild animals were originally understood as a manifestation of this recovery of paradisiacal innocence. As one of the early writers, Paul the Hermit, declared: "If anyone acquires purity, everything will submit to him as it did to Adam in paradise before the fall." (Quoted in Dom Anselm Stolz, *Théologie de la Mystique,* Chevetogne, 1947, p. 31)

If we admit Staretz Zosima's statement that paradise is something attainable because, after all, it is present within us and we have only to discover it there, we may still pause to question one part of his statement: "one has *only to wish to understand it,* and at once paradise will appear before us in all its beauty." That seems to be a little too easy. Much more is required than a simple velleity. Anyone can make a wish. But the kind of "wishing" that Zosima refers to here is something far beyond daydreaming and wishful thinking. It means, of course, a complete upheaval and transformation of one's whole life. One has to "wish" for this one realization alone and give up wishing for anything else. One has to forget the quest of every other "good." One has to devote himself with his whole heart and soul to the recovery of his "innocence." And yet, as Dr. Suzuki has so well pointed out, and as the Christian doctrine of grace teaches us in other terms, this cannot be the work of our own "self." It is useless for the "self" to try to "purify itself," or for the "self" to "make a place in itself" for God. The innocence and purity of heart which belong to paradise are a complete emptiness of self in which all is the work of God, the free and unpredictable expression of His love, the work of grace. In the purity of original innocence, all is done in us but without us, *in nobis et sine nobis*. But before we reach that level, we must also learn to work on the other level of "knowledge"—*scientia*—where grace works in us but "not without us"—*in nobis sed non sine nobis*.

Dr. Suzuki has, in his own terms, very aptly pointed out that it would be a serious error to think that one could hoist himself back by his own bootstraps into the state of innocence and go on blissfully with no further concern about the present life. Innocence does not cast out or destroy knowledge. The two must go together. That, indeed, was where many apparently spiritual men have failed. Some of them were so innocent that they had lost all contact with everyday reality of life in a struggling and complex world of men. But their's was not true innocence. It was fictitious, a perversion and frustration of the real spiritual life. It was the emptiness of the quietist, an emptiness that was merely blank and silly: an absence of knowledge without the presence of wisdom. It was the narcissistic ignorance of the baby, not the emptiness of the saint who is moved, without reflection or self-consciousness, by the grace of God.

At this point, however, I would like to question Dr. Suzuki's interpretation of the story of the "great hermit" who had the robbers arrested. I am tempted to wonder if there is not, in this reaction of his, a touch of what might be called "overcompensation." There is, in fact, quite a lot of Zen in this story of the robbers and of the "great hermit." At any rate, it is the kind of story a Western reader might be tempted to spot right away as having affinities with the spirit of Zen. And perhaps Dr. Suzuki is too much on his guard against such an interpretation which would, of course, tend toward the old accusation of antinomianism. Certainly the "great hermit" does not seem to have much respect for laws, jails and police.

But if we look at the story a little closer we find that the point is quite a different matter. No one is saying that robbers ought not to go to jail. What is pointed out is that hermits have no business sending them there. The robber should, certainly, respect property rights; but the hermit, consecrated to a life of poverty and "emptiness," has forfeited his right to be concerned with possessions, with property or with material security. On the contrary, if he is what he ought to be, he will do what Dr. Suzuki's farmer did, and help the robbers with a ladder. But no, these monks are spiritually sick. Far from being empty of themselves, they are full of themselves, they rise up in anger when their selfish interests are touched or even menaced. They revenge wrongs that are done to them because they are all bound up with a "self" that can be wronged and feel outraged. In the words of the "Path of Virtue" (*Dhammapada*):

> He verily is not an anchorite who oppresses others;
> He is not an ascetic who causes grief to another.

This is almost identical with one of the sayings of Abbot Pastor:

> "He who is quarrelsome is no monk; he who returns evil for evil is no monk; he who gets angry is no monk." (*The Wisdom of The Desert*, XLIX)

So the outraged hermits are in reality much more to blame than the robbers, because precisely it is people like these who cause poor men to become robbers. It is those who acquire inordinate possessions for themselves and defend them against others, who make it necessary for the others to steal in order to make a living. That at least is the idea of Abbot Poemen and in telling "great hermit" to let the robbers out of jail he was being neither antisocial nor sentimental; he was just giving his monks a lesson in poverty. They did not wish to know the paradise that was within them through detachment and purity of heart: but rather they wanted to keep themselves in darkness and defilement by their love of their own possessions and their own comfort. They did not want the "wisdom" that "tastes" the presence of God in freedom and emptiness, but the "knowledge" of "mine" and "thine" and of violated rights "vindicated" by recourse to the police and to torture.


## II

The fathers of the Church have interpreted man's creation in the "image of God" as a proof that he is capable of paradisiacal innocence and of contemplation, and that these are indeed the purpose of his creation. Man was made in order that in his emptiness and purity of heart he might mirror the purity and freedom of the invisible God and thus be perfectly one with Him. But the recovery of this paradise, which is always hidden within us at least as a possibility, is a matter of great practical difficulty. Genesis tells us that the way back to Paradise is barred by an angel with a flaming sword "turning every way." Yet that does not mean that the return is absolutely impossible. As St. Ambrose says: "All who wish to return to paradise must be tested by the fire." (*Oportet omnes per ignem probari quicumque ad paradisum redire desiderant. In Psalmum* 118, xx, 12. Quoted in Stolz, p. 32) The way from knowledge to innocence, or the purification of the heart, is a way of temptation and struggle. It is a matter of wrestling with supreme difficulties and overcoming obstacles that seem, and indeed are, beyond human strength.

Dr. Suzuki has not mentioned one of the main actors in the drama of the Fall: the devil. Buddhism certainly has a very definite concept of this personage (*Mara*—the tempter) and if ever there was a spirtuality more concerned with the devil than that of the Egyptian desert, it is the Buddhism of Tibet. In Zen, however, the devil appears relatively little. We see him occasionally in these "Sayings of the Fathers." But his presence is everywhere noted in the desert, which is indeed his refuge. The first and greatest of hermits, St. Anthony, is the classic type of the wrestler with the devil. The Desert Fathers invaded the devil's own exclusive territory in order, by overcoming him in singlehanded combat, to regain paradise.

Without attempting the delicate task of fully identifying this ubiquitous and evil spirit, let us remind ourselves that in the first pages of the Bible he appears as the one who offers man the "knowledge of good and evil" as something "better," superior and more "godlike" than the state of innocence and emptiness. And in the last pages of the Bible the devil is finally "cast out" when man is restored to unity with God in Christ. The significant point is that in these verses of the Apocalypse (12:10) the devil is called "the accuser of our brethren . . . who accused them before God day and night." In the Book of Job, the devil is not only the one who causes Job's sufferings, but it is understood that he also acts as a "tempter" through the moralizing of Job's friends.

The friends of Job appear on the scene as advisers and "consolers," offering Job the fruits of their moral scientia. But when Job insists that his sufferings have *no explanation* and that he cannot discover the reason for them through conventional ethical concepts, his friends turn into accusers, and curse Job as a sinner. Thus, instead of consolers, they become torturers by virtue of their very morality, and in so doing, while claiming to be advocates of God, they act as instruments of the devil.

In other words, the realm of knowledge or *scientia* is a realm where man is subject to the influence of the devil. This does nothing to alter the fact that knowledge is good and necessary. Nevertheless, even when our "science" does not fail us, it still tends to delude us. Its perspectives are not those of our inmost, spiritual nature. And at the same time we are constantly being misled by passion, attachment to self and by the "deceptions of the devil." The realm of knowledge is then a realm of alienation and peril, in which we are not our true selves and in which we are likely to become completely enslaved to the power of illusion. And this is true not only when we fall into sin but also to some extent even when we avoid it. The Desert Fathers realized that the most dangerous activity of the devil came into play against the monk only when he was morally perfect, that is, apparently "pure" and virtuous enough to be capable of spiritual pride. Then began the struggle with the last and subtlest of the attachments: the attachment to one's own spiritual excellence; the love of one's spiritualized, purified and "empty" self; the narcissism of the perfect, of the pseudo-saint and of the false mystic.

The only escape, as St. Anthony said, was humility. And the Desert Fathers' concept of humility corresponds very closely to the spiritual poverty Dr. Suzuki has just described for us. One must possess and retain absolutely nothing, not even a self in which he can receive angelic visitations, not even a selflessness he can be proud of. True sanctity is not the work of man purifying himself, it is God Himself present in His own transcendent light, which to us is emptiness.


III

Let us look more closely at two Patristic texts on science (*scientia*) or knowledge, as it occurred in the fall of Adam. St. Augustine says:

> "This science is described as the recognition of good and evil because the soul ought to reach out to what is beyond itself, that is to God, and to forget what is beneath itself, that is bodily pleasure. But if the soul, deserting God, turns in upon itself and wishes to enjoy its own spiritual power as though without God, it becomes inflated with pride, which is the beginning of all sin. And when it is thus punished for its sin, it learns by experience what a distance separates the good it has deserted and the evil into which it has fallen. This then is what it means to have tasted the fruit of the tree of the knowledge of good and evil." (*De Genesi contra Manichaeos,* ix. Migne, P.L., vol. 34, col. 203)

And again in another place:

> "When the soul deserts the wisdom (*sapientia*) of love, which is always unchanging and one, and desires knowledge (*scientia*) from the experience of temporal and changing things, it becomes puffed up rather than built up. And weighed down in this manner the soul falls away from blessedness as though by its own heaviness." (*De Trinitate* xii, 11. Migne, P.L., vol. 42, col. 1007)

A few brief words of comment will clarify this concept of "knowledge" and of its effects. First of all, the state in which man is created is one of un-selfconscious "reaching out" to what is metaphysically higher than himself, but nevertheless intimately present within his own being, so that he himself is hidden in God and united with Him. This is what, for St. Augustine, corresponds to the innocence of paradise and to "emptiness." The knowledge of good and evil begins with the fruition of sensible and temporal things for their own sakes, an act which makes the soul conscious of itself, and centers it on its own pleasure. It becomes aware of what is good and evil "for itself." As soon as this takes place, there is a complete change of perspective, and from unity or wisdom (identified with emptiness and purity) the soul now enters into a state of dualism. It is now aware of both itself and God, as separated beings. It now sees God as an object of desire or of fear, and is no longer lost in Him as in a transcendent subject. Furthermore it is aware of God as of an antagonistic and hostile being. And yet it is attracted to Him as to its highest good. But the experience of itself becomes a "weight" which gravitates away from God. Each act of self-affirmation increases the dualistic tension between self and God. Remember Augustine's dictum, *amor meus, pondus meum.* "My love is a weight, a gravitational force." As one loves temporal things, one gains an illusory substantiality and a selfhood which gravitates "downward," that is to say acquires a *need* for things lower in the scale of being than itself. It depends on these things for its own self-affirmation. In the end this gravitational pull becomes an enslavement to material and temporal cares, and finally to sin. Yet this weight itself is an illusion, a result of the "puffing up" of pride, a "swelling" without reality. The self that appears to be weighed down by its love and carried away to material things is, in fact, an unreal thing. Yet it retains an empirical existence of its own: it is what we think of as ourselves. And this empirical existence is strengthened by every act of selfish desire or fear. It is not the true self, the Christian person, the image of God stamped with the likeness of Christ. It is the false self, the disfigured image, the caricature, the emptiness that has swelled up and become full of itself, so as to create a kind of fictional substantiality for itself. Such is Augustine's commentary on the phrase of St. Paul: *scientia inflat.* "Knowledge puffeth up."

These two passages from St. Augustine are sufficiently good parallels to the process which Dr. Suzuki describes in the sentence, "Out of the Emptiness of the Mind a thought mysteriously arises and we have the world of multiplicities." I do not of course insist that St. Augustine is teaching Zen. Far from it! There remain deep and significant divergences which we need not study at this point. Let it suffice to have said that there are also certain important similarities, due in great part to the Platonism of St. Augustine.

Once we find ourselves in the state of "knowledge of good and evil" we have to accept the fact and understand our position, see it in relation to the innocence for which we were created, which we have lost and which we can regain. But in the meantime it is a question of treating knowledge and innocence as complementary realities. This was the most delicate problem confronting the Desert Fathers, and for many of them it led to disaster. They recognized the difference between "knowledge of good and evil" on the one hand, and innocence or emptiness on the other. But, as Dr. Suzuki has wisely observed, they ran the risk of oversimplified and abstract solutions. Too many of them wanted to get along simply with innocence without knowledge. In our *Sayings,* John the Dwarf is a case in point. He wants to reach a state in which there is no temptation, no further stirring of the slightest passion.[11] All this is nothing but a refinement of "knowledge." Instead of leading to innocence, it leads to the most quintessentially pure love of self. It leads to the creation of a pseudo-emptiness, an exquisitely purified self that is so perfect that it can rest in itself without any trace of crude reflection. Yet this is not emptiness: there remains a "self" that is the subject of purity and the possessor of emptiness. And this, as the Desert Fathers saw, is the final triumph of the subtle tempter. It leaves a man rooted and imprisoned in his pure self, a clever discerner of good and evil, of self and nonself, purity and impurity. But he is not innocent. He is a master of spiritual knowledge. And as such, he is still subject to accusation from the devil. Since he is *perfect,* he is subject to the greatest deception of all. If he were *innocent,* he would be free from deception.

The man who has truly found his spiritual nakedness, who has realized he is empty, is not a self that has *acquired* emptiness or *become* empty. He just "is empty from the beginning," as Dr. Suzuki has observed. Or, to put it in the more affective terms of St. Augustine and St. Bernard, he "loves with a pure love." That is to say he loves with a purity and freedom that spring spontaneously and directly from the fact that he has fully recovered the divine likeness, and is now fully his true self because he is lost in God. He is one with God and identified with God and hence knows nothing of any ego in himself. All he knows is love. As St.

[11] "Abbot Pastor said that Abbot John the Dwarf had prayed to the Lord and the Lord had taken away all his passions, so that he became impassible. And in this condition he went to one of the elders and said: You see before you a man who is completely at rest and has no more temptations. The elder said: Go and pray to the Lord to command some struggle to be stirred up in you, for the soul is matured only in battles. And when the temptations started up again he did not pray that the struggle be taken away from him, but only said: Lord, give me strength to get through the fight."—*The Wisdom of The Desert,* XCI.

Bernard says: "He who loves thus, simply loves, and knows nothing else but love." *Qui amat, amat et aliud novit nihil.*

Whether or not the Desert Fathers were fully articulate in expressing this kind of emptiness, they certainly strove for it. And their instrument in opening the subtle locks of spiritual deception was the virtue of *discretio*. It was discretion that St. Anthony called the most important of all the virtues in the desert. Discretion had taught him the value of simple manual labor. Discretion taught the fathers that purity of heart did not consist simply in fasting and self-maceration. Discretion—otherwise called the discernment of spirits—is indeed germane to the realm of knowledge, since it does distinguish between good and evil. But it exercises its functions in the light of innocence and in reference to emptiness. It judges not in terms of abstract standards so much as in terms of inner purity of heart. Discretion makes judgments and indicates choices, but the judgment and choice always point in the direction of emptiness, or purity of heart. Discretion is a function of humility, and therefore it is a branch of knowledge that lies beyond the reach of diabolical comment and perversion. (See Cassian, Conference II, *De Discretione.* Migne, P.L., vol. 49, c. 523 ff.)

## IV

John Cassian, in his reports of the "conferences" he heard among the Desert Fathers, lays down the fundamental rule of desert spirituality. What is the purpose and end of the monastic life? Such is the subject of the first conference.

The answer is that the monastic life has a twofold purpose. It must lead the monk first to an intermediate end, and then to an ultimate and final state of completion. The intermediate end, or *scopos,* is what we have been discussing as purity of heart, roughly corresponding to Dr. Suzuki's term "emptiness." That heart is pure which is *"perfectum ac mundissimum"* (perfect and most pure), that is to say completely free of alien thoughts and desires. The concept, in actual fact, corresponds rather to the Stoic *apatheia* than to Zen "suchness." But at any rate there is a close relationship. It is the *quies,* or rest, of contemplation—the state of being free from all images and concepts which disturb and occupy the soul. It is the favorable climate for *theologia,* the highest contemplation, which excludes even the purest and most spiritual of ideas and admits no concepts whatever. It knows God not by concepts or visions, but only by "unknowing." This is the language of Evagrius Ponticus, severely intellectual, a fact which brings him closer to Zen than the more affective theologians of prayer like St. Maximus and St. Gregory of Nyssa. Cassian himself, though close to Evagrius and sympathetic with him, nevertheless gives a characteristically Christian affective balance to the concept of purity of heart, and insists that it is to be defined simply as "perfect charity" or a love of God unmixed with any return upon self. This qualification might conceivably constitute a significant difference between Christian "purity of heart" and the "emptiness" of Zen, but the relations between the two concepts should be further studied.

One thing, and this is most important, remains to be said. Purity of heart is not the *ultimate end* of the monk's striving in the desert. It is only a step towards it. We have said above that Paradise is not yet heaven. Paradise is not the final goal of the spiritual life. It is, in fact, only a return to the true beginning. It is a "fresh start." The monk who has realized in himself purity of heart, and has been restored, in some measure, to the innocence lost by Adam, has still not ended his journey. He is only ready to begin. He is ready for a new work "which eye hath not seen, ear hath not heard, nor hath it entered into the heart of man to conceive." Purity of heart, says Cassian, is the intermediate end of the spiritual life. But the ultimate end is the Kingdom of God. This is a dimension which does not enter into the realm of Zen.

One might argue that this simply overturns all that has been said about emptiness, and brings us back into a state of dualism, and therefore to "knowledge of good and evil," duality between man and God, etc. Such is by no means the case. Purity of heart establishes man in a state of unity and emptiness in which he is one with God. But this is the necessary preparation not for further struggle between good and evil, but for the real work of God which is revealed in the Bible: the work of the *new creation,* the resurrection from the dead, the restoration of all things in Christ. This is the real dimension of Christianity, the eschatalogical dimension which is peculiar to it, and which has no parallel in Buddhism. The world was created without man, but the new creation which is the true Kingdom of God is to be the work of God in and through man. It is to be the great, mysterious, theandric work of the Mystical Christ, the New Adam, in whom all men as "one Person" or one "Son of God" will transfigure the cosmos and offer it resplendent to the Father. Here, in this transfiguration, will take place the apocalyptic marriage between God and His creation, the final and perfect consummation of which no mortal mysticism is able to dream and which is barely foreshadowed in the symbols and images of the last pages of the Apocalypse.

Here, of course, we are back in the realm of concept and image. To think about these things, to speculate on them, is, perhaps, to depart from "emptiness." But it is an activity of faith that belongs to our realm of knowledge, and conditions us for a superior and more vigilant innocence: the innocence of the wise virgins who wait with lighted lamps, with an emptiness that is enkindled by the glory of the Divine Word and enflamed with the presence of the Holy Spirit. That glory and that presence are not objects which "enter into" emptiness to "fill" it. They are nothing else but God's own "suchness."


FINAL REMARKS

*by Daisetz T. Suzuki*

I am not well acquainted with all the Christian literature produced by the learned, talented and logically-minded theologians who have endeavored to intellectually clarify their experiences, and therefore, the comments I make on Christianity, its doctrines and traditions, may miss the mark altogether. I would like to say that there are two types of mentality which fundamentally differ one from the other: (1) affective, personal and dualistic, and (2) nonaffective, nonpersonal and nondualistic. Zen belongs to the latter and Christianity naturally to the former. The fundamental difference may be illustrated by the conception of "emptiness."

Father Merton's emptiness, when he uses this term, does not go far and deep enough, I am afraid. I do not know who first made the distinction between the Godhead and God as Creator. This distinction is strikingly illustrative. Father Merton's emptiness is still on the level of God as Creator and does not go up to the Godhead. So is John Cassian's. The latter has, according to Father Merton, "God's own 'suchness'" for the ultimate end of a monkish life. In my view, this way of interpreting "suchness" is the emptiness of God as Creator, and not of the Godhead. Zen emptiness is not the emptiness of nothingness, but the emptiness of fullness in which there is "no gain, no loss, no increase, no decrease," in which this equation takes place: zero = infinity. The Godhead is no other than this equation. In other words, when God as Creator came out of the Godhead he did not leave the Godhead behind. He has the Godhead with him all along while engaging in the work of creation. Creation is continuous, going on till the end of time, which has really no ending and therefore no beginning. For creation is out of inexhaustible nothingness.

Paradise has never been lost and therefore is never regained. As Staretz Zosima says, according to Father Merton, as soon as one wishes for it, that is to say, as soon as I become conscious of the fact, Paradise is right away with me, and the experience is the foundation on which the kingdom of heaven is built. Eschatology is something never realizable and yet realized at every moment of our life. We see it always ahead of us though we are in reality always in it. This is the delusion we are conditioned to have as beings in time or rather as "becomings" in time. The delusion ceases to be one the very moment we experience all this. It is the Great Mystery, intellectually speaking. In Christian terms, it is Divine Wisdom. The strange thing, however, is: when we experience it we cease to ask questions about it, we accept it, we just live it. Theologians, dialecticians and existentialists may go on discussing the matter, but the ordinary people inclusive of all of us who are outsiders live "the mystery." A Zen Master was once asked:

Q. What is Tao? (We may take Tao as meaning the ultimate truth or reality.)

A. It is one's everyday mind.

Q. What is one's everyday mind?

A. When tired, you sleep; when hungry, you eat.

*by Thomas Merton*

The points Dr. Suzuki has raised are of the highest importance. First of all it is clear that the strongly personalistic tone of Christian mysticism, even when it is "apophatic," generally seems to prohibit a full equation with Zen experience. In cautiously walking around the distinction between "God and Godhead" I am simply avoiding a thorny theological problem. This distinction, of a clearly dualistic character, has been technically condemned by the Church. What Dr. Suzuki (in his qualified statement following Eckhart and the Rhenish mystics) wants to express has to be treated in other terms. The theologians of the Oriental Church seek to state it by their distinction between the "divine energies" (through and in which God "works" outside Himself) and the "divine substance" which is beyond all knowledge and experience. John Ruysbroeck resolves it down to the distinction between the Trinity of Persons and the Unity of Nature. Whether or not this is satisfactory I cannot discuss here. The climax of Ruysbroeck's mysticism is an "emptiness without manner." By "manner" Ruysbroeck seems to mean a qualified mode of being that can be grasped and conceived intellectually. We know "God" in our concepts of His essence and attributes, but "beyond all manner" (and therefore beyond all conceiving) in His transcendent, ineffable reality which to Dr. Suzuki is "Godhead" or "suchness." If this is what he means, I think his view is thoroughly acceptable and I heartily concur with it. Ruysbroeck says: "For God's *impenetrable lack of manner* is so dark and without manner that in itself it comprehends all the Divine manners . . . and in the abyss of God's namelessness it makes a Divine delectation. In this there is a delectable passing over and a *flowing-away and a sinking-down into the essential nakedness,* with all the Divine names and all manners and all living reason which has its image in the mirror of divine truth; all these *fall away into this simple nakedness wanting manner and without reason."* This "essential nakedness" I think corresponds to Dr. Suzuki's emptiness of the "Godhead" more clearly than the quote from Cassian. But certainly Ruysbroeck has gone further on the road toward Zen than the Desert Fathers and Cassian ever did. Ruysbroeck is a pupil of Eckhart who seems to Dr. Suzuki to be the Christian mystic closest to Zen.

If in my own exposition I have not spoken so much of "sinking down into the essential nakedness" of God it is not because I have insisted on man's awareness of God as Creator but rather, at least implicitly, on man's dependence upon God as Savior and giver of grace. Now of course in speaking of a "giver," a "gift" and a "receiver" I am speaking in terms of knowledge more than of wisdom. And this is inevitable, just as, according to Dr. Suzuki, we are inevitably involved in ethical concern in our present condition. But the ethical is not ultimate. Beyond all consideration of right and wrong is the simplicity, the purity, the emptiness or the "suchness" for which there is and can be no wrong because it cannot coexist with moral deordination. As soon as there is sin there is the "self" that affirms its own egocentricity and destroys the purity of true freedom. At the same time, it seems to me that from a Christian viewpoint supreme purity, emptiness, freedom and "suchness" still have the character of a *free gift* of love, and perhaps it is this freedom, this *giving without reason, without limit, without return, without self-conscious afterthought,* that is the real secret of God who "is love." I cannot develop the idea at this point but it seems to me that in actual fact the purest Christian equivalent to Dr. Suzuki's formula zero = infinity is to be sought precisely in the basic Christian intuition of divine mercy. Not grace as a reified substance given to us by God from without, but grace precisely as emptiness, as freedom, as liberality, as gift. I would like to add that Dr. Suzuki has approached the subject from this same viewpoint in his extremely interesting essays on the *Nembutsu,* and "Pure Land Buddhism."[12] This is no longer Zen, and it is much closer to Christianity than Zen is. It is in so far as "emptiness" and "nakedness" are also *pure gift* that in Christian terms they equal fullness. But lest the idea of gift be interpreted in a divisive "dualistic" sense, let us remember that God is His own Gift, that the Gift of the Spirit is the gift of freedom and emptiness. His giving emerges from His Godhead, and as Ruysbroeck says, it is through the Spirit that we plunge back into the essential nakedness of the Godhead where "the depths themselves remain uncomprehended. . . . This is the dark silence in which all lovers are lost."

Hence I certainly agree with Dr. Suzuki in rejecting an emptiness that is merely empty, and merely a counterpart of some imagined fullness standing over against it in metaphysical isolation. No, when we are empty we become capable of fullness (which has never been absent from us). Paradise has been lost insofar as we have become involved in complexity and wound up in ourselves so that we are estranged from our own freedom and our own simplicity. Paradise cannot be opened to us except by a free gift of the divine mercy. Yet it is true to say that Paradise is always present within us, since God Himself is present, though perhaps inaccessible.

I think Dr. Suzuki's intuition about the eschatalogical nature of reality is vivid and very profound and it impresses me as much more deeply Christian than perhaps he himself imagines. Here too I would tend to see this reality from the point of view of freedom and of "gift." We are in the "fullness

[12] For instance, "Passivity in the Buddhist Life" in *Essays in Zen Buddhism:* Series II, London, 1958.

137

of time" and all is "given" into our hands. We imagine that we are traveling toward an end that is to come, and in a sense that is true. Christianity moves in an essentially historical dimension toward the "restoration of all things in Christ." Yet with Christ's conquest of death and the sending of the Holy Spirit that restoration has already been accomplished. What remains is for it to be made manifest. But we must always remember, as did the Desert Fathers, that *"now* is the judgment of the world." To one who does not experience the reality behind the concept, this remains an illusion. To one who has seen it, the most obvious thing is to do what Dr. Suzuki suggests: to live one's ordinary life. In the words of the first Christians, to praise God and to take one's food "in simplicity of heart." The simplicity referred to here is the complete absence of all legalistic preoccupation about right and wrong foods, right and wrong ways of eating, right and wrong ways of living. "When tired, you sleep, when hungry you eat." For the Buddhist, life is a static and ontological fullness. For the Christian it is a dynamic gift, a fullness of love. There are many differences in the doctrines of the two religions, but I am deeply gratified to find, in this dialogue with Dr. Suzuki, that thanks to his penetrating intuitions into Western mystical thought, we can so easily and agreeably communicate with one another on the deepest and most important level. I feel that in talking to him I am talking to a "fellow citizen," to one who, though his beliefs in many respects differ from mine, shares a common spiritual climate. This unity of outlook and purpose is supremely significant.

# POSTFACE

This book is really back to front. The most recently written essay is the one that comes first. Most of the material belongs to the last three or four years. The dialogue with Suzuki goes back further—about ten years. I was tempted to cut out my own "final remarks" in the dialogue because they are so confusing. Not that they are "wrong" in the sense of "false" or "erroneous," but because any attempt to handle Zen in theological language is bound to miss the point. If I leave these remarks where they are, I do so as an example of how *not* to approach Zen.

On the other hand, to reverse the order and put each article in its proper chronological position would also be beside the point. If the reader is uneasy with these last few pages, let him go back and read the Author's Note at the beginning. It might clear the air. If he has begun by reading the Postface, as some might do, then let him realize that he is free to read the rest of the book in whatever order he likes.

One more remark. The quote from Wittgenstein ("Don't think, look") must not be misconstrued. The Zen intuition which sees reality in ordinary life is in fact poles apart from the canonization of "ordinary speech" by linguistic analysis. True, they both reject mystifications and ideological superstructures which, in attempting to account for what is in front of us, get in its way. But I, for one, completely agree with Herbert Marcuse's analysis of the "one-dimensional thinking" in which the very rationality and exactitude of technological society and its various justifications, add up to one more total mystification. It is possible that some people understand Zen in a sort of positivistic sense (and their repudiation of "mysticism" is then merely "square"). But Zen cannot be grasped as long as one remains passively conformed to *any* cultural or social imperatives, whether ideological, sociological, or what have you. Zen is not one-dimensional, and its repudiation of dualistic thinking does not mean the acceptance of a totalitarian culture (though a fatal misunderstanding of it might in fact promote an adjustment to fascism, and has in fact done so in a few cases). Zen implies a breakthrough, an explosive liberation from one-dimensional conformism, a recovery of unity which is not the suppression of opposites but a simplicity beyond opposites. To exist and function in the world of opposites while experiencing that world in terms of a primal simplicity does imply if not a formal metaphysic, at least a ground of metaphysical intuition. This means a totally different perspective than that which dominates our society—and enables it to dominate us.

Hence the Zen saying: before I grasped Zen, the mountains were nothing but mountains and the rivers nothing but rivers. When I got into Zen, the mountains were no longer mountains and the rivers no longer rivers. But when I understood Zen, the mountains were only mountains and the rivers only rivers.

The point is that facts are not just plain facts. There is a dimension where the bottom drops out of the world of factuality and of the ordinary. Western industrial culture is in the curious position of having simultaneously reached the climax of an entire totalitarian rationality of organization and of complete absurdity and self-contradiction. Existentialists and a few others have noticed the absurdity. But the majority persist in seeing only the rational machinery against which no protest avails: because, after all, it is "rational," and it is "a fact." So, too, is the internal contradiction.

The thing about Zen is that it pushes contradictions to their ultimate limit where one has to choose between madness and innocence. And Zen suggests that we may be driving toward one or the other on a cosmic scale. Driving toward them because, one way or the other, as madmen or innocents, we are already there.

It might be good to open our eyes and *see*.

# New Directions Paperbooks—A Partial Listing